the Wood Stash PROJECT BOOK

KERRY PIERCE

**POPULAR
WOODWORKING
BOOKS**

CINCINNATI, OHIO
www.popularwoodworking.com

READ THIS IMPORTANT SAFETY NOTICE

To prevent accidents, keep safety in mind while you work. The tool guards in some photos have been removed for clarity. Use the safety guards installed on power equipment; they are for your protection. When working on power equipment, keep fingers away from saw blades, wear safety goggles to prevent injuries from flying wood chips and sawdust, wear headphones to protect your hearing and consider installing a dust vacuum to reduce the amount of airborne sawdust in your woodshop. Don't wear loose clothing, such as neckties or shirts with loose sleeves, or jewelry, such as rings, necklaces or bracelets, when working on power equipment. Tie back long hair to prevent it from getting caught in your equipment. People who are sensitive to certain chemicals should check the chemical content of any product before using it. The authors and editors who compiled this book have tried to make the contents as accurate and correct as possible. Plans, illustrations, photographs and text have been carefully checked. All instructions, plans and projects should be carefully read, studied and understood before beginning construction. Due to the variability of local conditions, construction materials, skill levels, etc., neither the author nor Popular Woodworking Books assumes any responsibility for any accidents, injuries, damages or other losses incurred resulting from the material presented in this book. Prices listed for supplies and equipment were current at the time of publication and are subject to change. All glass shelving should have all edges polished and must be tempered. Untempered glass shelves will shatter and can cause serious bodily injury. Tempered shelves are very strong and if they do break, they will just crumble, minimizing personal injury.

METRIC CONVERSION CHART

to convert	to	multiply by
Inches	Centimeters	2.54
Centimeters	Inches	0.4
Feet	Centimeters	30.5
Centimeters	Feet	0.03
Yards	Meters	0.9
Meters	Yards	1.1
Sq. Inches	Sq. Centimeters	6.45
Sq. Centimeters	Sq. Inches	0.16
Sq. Feet	Sq. Meters	0.09
Sq. Meters	Sq. Feet	10.8
Sq. Yards	Sq. Meters	0.8
Sq. Meters	Sq. Yards	1.2
Pounds	Kilograms	0.45
Kilograms	Pounds	2.2
Ounces	Grams	28.4
Grams	Ounces	0.035

The Wood Stash Project Book. Copyright © 2002 by Kerry Pierce. Manufactured in Singapore. All rights reserved. No part of this book may be reproduced in any form or by any electronic or mechanical means, including information storage and retrieval systems, without permission in writing from the publisher, except by a reviewer, who may quote brief passages in a review. Published by Popular Woodworking Books, an imprint of F&W Publications, Inc., 4700 East Galbraith Road, Cincinnati, Ohio, 45236. First edition.

Visit our Web site at www.popularwoodworking.com for more information and resources for woodworkers.

Other fine Popular Woodworking Books are available from your local bookstore or direct from the publisher.

06   05   04   03   02   5   4   3   2   1

Library of Congress Cataloging-in-Publication Data
Pierce, Kerry.
    The wood stash project book / by Kerry Pierce.
        p. cm.
    Includes bibliographical references and index.
    ISBN 1-55870-600-3 (alk. paper)
    1. Woodwork--Amateurs' manuals. I. Title.

    TT185.P5885 2002
    684'.08--dc21

                            2001059336

Edited by Jennifer Churchill & Jenny Ziegler
Designed by Brian Roeth
Page layout by Tari Sasser
Lead photography by Al Parrish
Step-by-step photography by Kerry Pierce
Production coordinated by Mark Griffin
Measured drawings by Kevin Pierce
Tool drawings by Kerry Pierce
Acquisitions editor: Jim Stack

SUPPLIERS

Woodcraft
560 Airport Industrial Park
P. O. Box 1686
Parkersburg, WV 26102
(800) 225-1153
www.woodcraft.com
magnets, clock supplies

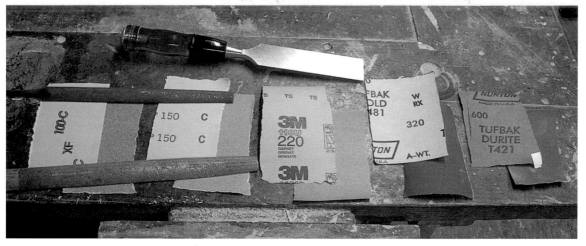

step 1 These are the finish preparation tools I use in my shop. The rasp and butt chisel (used as a scraper) perform the preliminary work. The use of a succession of sanding grits produces a smooth surface for finishing.

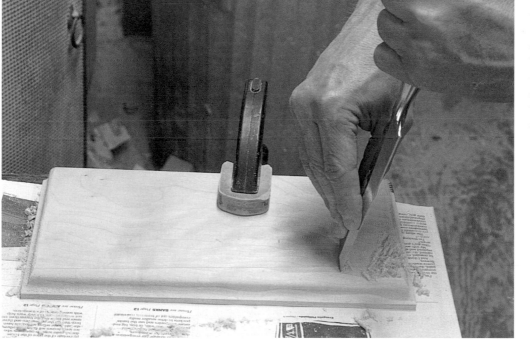

step 2 A butt chisel used as a scraper can remove a paper thin shaving of wood, reducing the surface much more quickly than with sandpaper. Also, the butt chisel leaves behind a smooth surface of sheared fibers, rather than the rough surface of torn fibers left by coarse sandpaper.

step 3 When sanding large, flat surfaces like the bottom of this shelf, I wrap my sandpaper around a block of wood. The flat contact surface on the bottom of that block of wood prevents the kind of channels that can be eroded into a surface by coarse sandpaper gripped in the fingers.

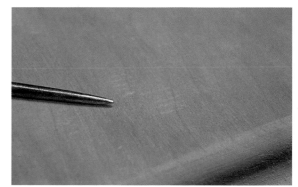

step 4 The sanding process can bring to light hidden areas of planer tear-out because the lighter-colored sanding dust settles in those torn-out areas. One such area is just above the tip of this scratch awl. Another sits below that to the right of the scratch awl tip. These should be scraped before any more sanding is done.

step 5 A bit of sandpaper folded into a tight roll makes it easier to get into the dips and hollows of moulded edges.

step 6 You can apply the finish with a synthetic-bristle brush.

step 7 Working with a little Water-lox poured into a coffee can, slather on a coat of finish. Neatness isn't important. Neither are brush marks. Coverage is the only consideration.

step 8 I use little triangular rips to keep finished objects raised so that air can circulate all around them.

step 9   After the finish has begun to get a little tacky, wipe the surfaces thoroughly with a clean rag. This leaves just a thin film of finish on the wood, eliminating any need for concern about brush marks and runs. However, particularly on end-grain surfaces, the surplus finish sometimes will migrate to the surface after it's been wiped, causing little bubbles like these seen here on the surface of a checker. Although later sanding will remove most of these bubbles, try to wipe them away before the finish has had a chance to set.

step 10   The next day, sand all finished surfaces with 600-grit wet/dry paper. Periodic dips in a can of paint thinner keep the paper from getting clogged up.

step 11   Apply the second coat of finish in exactly the same way you applied the first coat. After the second coat has dried, apply a coat of paste wax.

step 12   After the wax has dried, buff the surfaces with a soft cloth to bring out the luster in the wax.

cherry-wood vase

This cherry-wood vase will give you a chance to create an attractive exterior curve on a turned vessel without struggling with the difficulties of excavating the interior of a form having a narrow, difficult-to-get-tools-into neck. This is because the opening of the vase's neck needs to be only large enough to accept the stalk of a dried weed or flower.

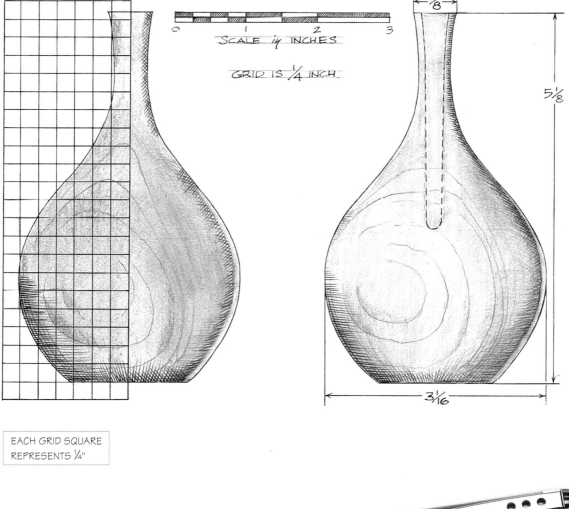

SCALE in INCHES

GRID IS ¼ INCH

5⅛

⅝

3¹⁄₁₆

EACH GRID SQUARE
REPRESENTS ¼"

materials list
cherry-wood vase

inches

QUANTITY	DIMENSIONS T W L
1 square pc.	$3^{1}/_{16}$ x $5^{1}/_{8}$

millimeters

QUANTITY	DIMENSIONS T W L
1 square pc.	78mm x 130mm

step 1 The process of designing a piece moves forward from what are often very crude beginnings to (hopefully) ever more refined variations. In the case of this particular cherry-wood vase, I started with a desire to use some short, thick pieces of curly maple and cherry I had been hanging on to for several years because they were just too nice to throw away. The sketch shown here presents the idea in its first incarnation. The curly-maple vase at right is my first attempt to turn that sketch into a finished form. I kept that curly-maple vase in the shop for several weeks, and I liked it less each time I saw it. I decided then to try the vase again, this time with the block of cherry shown on the left, hoping to produce a more pleasing result the second time around.

step 2 Begin by cutting an X from corner to corner into the end grain of the turning blank, cutting that X on the end from which you will eventually turn the narrow end of the vase. The point on the lathe's drive center will enter the blank where the two saw cuts cross, and the drive center's spurs will fit into the cuts. (A different, easier alternative to this method of X'ing is shown in chapter five.) Although it doesn't matter much when turning something so short, the general rule is that the end of the spindle that is to be turned to the smallest diameter should be on the end that mates with the drive center, because that is the most stable end of the lathe. The center on the opposite end of the turning blank can be found by drawing pencil lines from corner to corner. The point of the tail stock center will enter that end grain where those pencil lines cross.

step 3 Create a band saw cradle by cutting a notch, with the faces of that notch 90° apart. Draw lines on the four faces of the turning blank approximately 1" from the corners. Holding the turning blank in the cradle as shown, feed the blank into the band saw blade along the lines. The result will be an eight-sided turning blank that will be easier to rough in on the lathe than the four-sided turning blank with which you began.

TIP I'm left handed. If you're right handed, you will feel more comfortable holding your tools in your right hand.

step 4 Use a large roughing gouge — the gouge shown here is 1⅛" — to knock off the corners of your turning blank.

step 5 Holding the gouge securely against the tool rest, bring it into the work. A slow lathe speed is better at this early stage. You can change to a higher speed once the blank has been turned to a cylinder.

step 6 After you have created a cylinder, set the roughing gouge aside and move to a ½" or ¾" spindle gouge.

step 7 Create the rounded bottom and the narrowed top by making repeated passes with the spindle gouge.

step 8 Stop from time to time to assess the curve you're creating. Although the specific measurements of that curve can vary from vase to vase, each one should result in a pleasing S curve that runs from the base of the vase all the way to the top of the neck.

step 9 Create the curve's final line with sandpaper. Cloth-backed is best because of its durability. Begin with a fairly coarse grit, perhaps 80–100. Then switch to 150, and finish with 220. As you did when using the spindle gouge, stop from time to time during the sanding to check the line you're creating. This is particularly important with the coarser grits, which can very rapidly remove material from your vase.

step 10 With a ½" paring chisel held bevel-side down on the tool rest, define the top of the vase's neck. (A parting tool is a better choice here, but on the day I turned this vase my parting tool was hiding from me, so I improvised.)

step 11 Wrap the vase in an old towel and gently clamp it in your vise. Then cut away the waste with a fine-toothed backsaw.

step 12 With a sharp chisel, pare away the excess just below the saw cut.

step 14 Using a ¼" bit, bore a deep — 2½" to 3½" — hole in the center of the opening you created earlier.

step 13 With a ³⁄₁₆" drill bit, first bore a shallow hole — ¾" to 1" — into the end grain of the neck. Although you need to be careful not to penetrate the sidewalls of the neck, it isn't essential to hit dead center. Once that starter hole has been drilled, use the drill bit as if it were a Dremel tool to abrade away the neck's interior. The object here is to create a graceful, tapered opening with sidewalls of a consistent thickness.

Lathe tools can be taken directly from the grinder to the lathe, without any honing. It is important, however, to get a sharp hollow-ground edge on these tools. To do this, I simply adjust the rest on my grinder to the appropriate angle, lay the body of the tool on that rest and grind, rotating the tool past the wheel as I grind.

step 15 Refine the drill work with a small-diameter rasp and a bit of sandpaper.

step 16 The finished opening should have a consistent wall diameter and a graceful taper leading down into the ¼" hole bored on the drill press.

step 17 I think the vase on the right is more attractive than the earlier version on the left.

faceted wooden beads

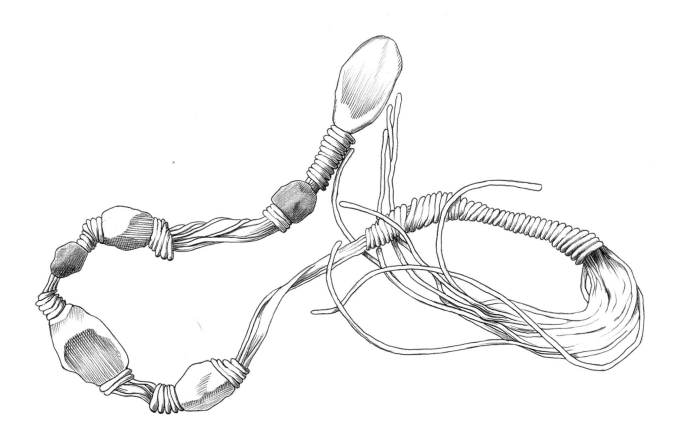

If your shop is like mine, you have, tucked away in a corner somewhere, an armload of hardwood rips you can't bear to throw away even though they're too thin or too narrow to actually use. Maybe you dust them off from time to time and sort through them, setting some aside to be chopped up into kindling. Or maybe, if you're like me, after a little consideration you eventually put them back into their dusty corner because they're walnut or curly maple or some exotic species you can't identify and can't remember ever having used. Don't despair. The cavalry has arrived. Here's your chance to put those rips to good use.

step 1 Choose a variety of colors — I picked maple, walnut and cherry — but if you don't have a variety of colorful species in your stash of rips, choose a single light-colored species, and later you can soak some of the beads in different shades of aniline dye to get the hues and values you want. Square a selection of these rips with repeated passes through the planer. You can do this with a hand plane if you don't have a planer. This is one project that doesn't require perfectly dimensioned stock.

step 2 Cut them into short lengths. I would recommend that you not attempt accurate sizing. One of the most appealing features of these beads is their essential randomness.

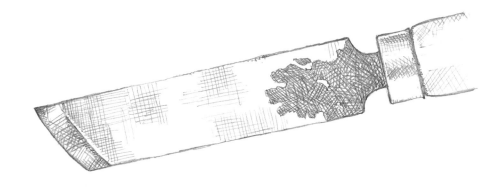

step 3 Fix a wood file in your vise. Smooth the saw marks from the end grain by repeatedly passing those end-grain surfaces across the file, in this manner creating smooth end-grain facets that will reflect light much like the side-grain facets you will cut later with your paring chisel.

step 4 To cut the facets, hold an individual bead against your bench top, then pare away the corners with a sharp chisel. Continue rotating the bead and paring away corners until you get a bead that looks right. Then, apply your finish without sanding, because any sanding will soften the edges where the facets meet and dull the reflected light.

step 5 Holding a bead in a pair of pliers, bore the ¼" through-hole (which will later receive a chain, string or cord) on the drill press. Again, don't worry about hitting dead center. These beads look best when each is distinctly different from every other bead. If you don't have a drill press, just fix the beads in your vise and use a handheld drill.

cherry key cache

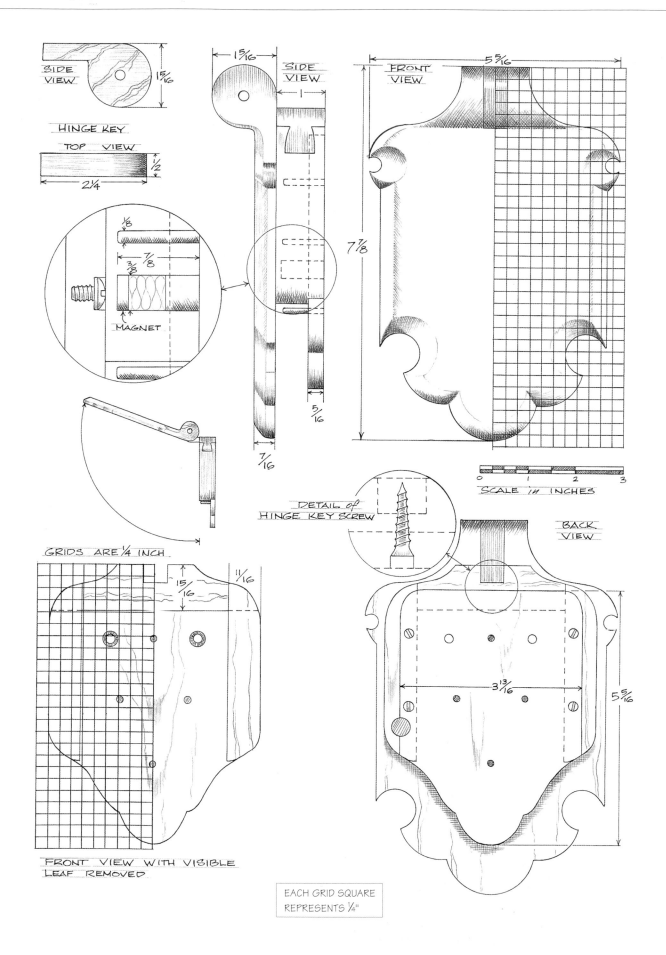

SIDE
VIEW

1 5/16

15/16

HINGE KEY

TOP   VIEW

1/2

2 1/4

SIDE
VIEW

1

1/8

7/8

3/8

MAGNET

DETAIL of
HINGE KEY SCREW

FRONT
VIEW

5 5/16

7 7/8

5/16

7/16

0   1   2   3

SCALE IN INCHES

BACK
VIEW

GRIDS ARE 1/4 INCH

15/16

11/16

3 13/16

5 5/16

FRONT VIEW WITH VISIBLE
LEAF REMOVED

EACH GRID SQUARE
REPRESENTS 1/4"

This project, which is small enough to be built from a half-dozen pieces of scrap, consists of a hinge, the hidden leaf of which contains a cubbyhole just large enough for four sets of keys. But in spite of the project's simplicity and its diminutive size, it offers the woodworker several very satisfying challenges; some simple but attractive carving, the creation of a set of hand-cut dovetails, and the construction of a functioning all-wood hinge.

materials list
cherry key cache

inches

ITEM	QUANTITY	DIMENSIONS T W L
Visible leaf	1 pc.	$1^5/_{16}$ x $5^5/_{16}$ x $7^7/_8$
Back/hidden leaf	1 pc.	$5/_{16}$ x $3^{13}/_{16}$ x $5^5/_{16}$
Side frame segs.	2 pcs.	$^{11}/_{16}$ x 1 x 4
Top frame seg.	1 pc.	1 x 1 x $4^1/_2$
Hinge key	1 pc.	$^1/_2$ x $1^{15}/_{16}$ x $2^1/_4$
Key pegs	4 pcs.	$^1/_8$ x $^7/_8$
Hinge pin	1 pc.	$^1/_4$ x $1^7/_8$
Hinge-key screws	4 pcs.	#6 x 1"
Hidden-leaf back screws	4 pcs.	#4 x $^3/_4$"
Rare earth magnet*	1 pcs.	$^3/_8$" diameter
Sheet-metal screw catch plate	1pc.	#6 x $^3/_8$"
Wood plug	1 pc.	$^3/_8$" x $^3/_8$"

*This includes $^9/_{16}$" of width to allow for the box's three tiers to be cut apart.

millimeters

ITEM	QUANTITY	DIMENSIONS T W L
Visible leaf	1 pc.	33 x 135 x 200
Back/hidden leaf	1 pc.	8 x 97 x 135
Side frame segs.	2 pcs.	18 x 25 x 102
Top frame seg.	1 pc.	25 x 25 x 115
Hinge key	1 pc.	13 x 49 x 64
Key pegs	4 pcs.	3 x 22
Hinge pin	1 pc.	6 x 47
Hinge-key screws	4 pcs.	#6 x 25mm
Hidden-leaf back screws	4 pcs.	#4 x 19mm
Rare earth magnet*	1 pc.	10mm diameter
Sheet-metal screw catch plate	1pc.	#6 x 10mm
Wood plug	1 pc.	10mm x 10mm

*This includes 14mm of width to allow for the box's three tiers to be cut apart.

step 1 Begin by ripping, jointing and cutting to length the stock for the visible hinge. Then check that at least one edge is perpendicular to the stock's two faces.

step 2 Make a final check that the faces are parallel to the band saw blade when the perpendicular edge of the stock rests on the band saw table.

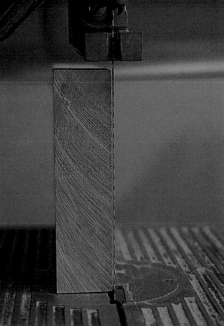

step 3 Mark the resawing lines on the edge opposite the one you've established as perpendicular to the stock's two faces. The perpendicular face must rest on the saw table.

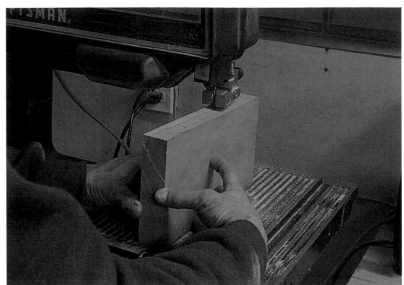

step 4 Carefully feed the stock into the band saw blade. Although a ½" (or wider) blade would be ideal for resawing the straight part of the visible leaf, the roll at the top has too small a radius to be cut with a ½" blade. I recommend a ¼" blade for the entire operation. However, with such a narrow blade used on such a thick cut, it's important to feed the material past the blade very gently to avoid putting enough stress on the blade to encourage it to wander.

step 5 With a block plane, clean up the roll of wood at the top of the visible leaf. When you're working with straight-grained material and a sharp plane it's possible to cut very cleanly across the grain.

step 6 With a jack plane, clean and level the flat resawn portion of the visible leaf. If you don't have a jack plane, your block plane can be used here, too.

step 7 Because a jack plane (or a block plane) can't cut right next to the wood roll, use a wide butt chisel to clean up that area. Properly sharpened, this tool makes a first-class scraper when it is pulled toward you under pressure with the bevel facing away.

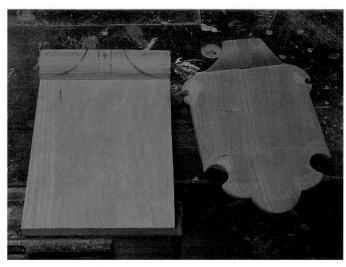

step 8 I used a short length of rattan splint as a straightedge to mark the notch for the hinge key. Any straight, flexible material will do.

step 9 Sketch in the curves on the wood roll freehand. Don't be concerned about achieving drawing perfection. This line will be refined as you work your way through the shaping processes. A finished leaf is visible on the right.

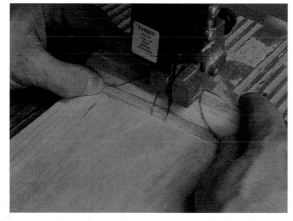

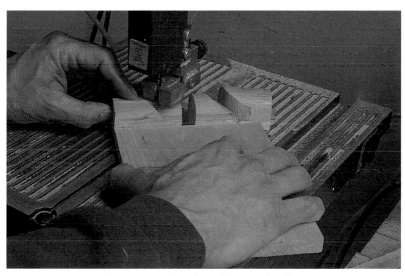

step 10 Stop the notch cuts as soon as the band saw blade has pushed loose a little noodle of wood, but before that noodle has been separated from the wood roll. That will keep you from cutting the notch too deeply.

step 11 Cut away the scrap on the sides of the wood roll.

step 12 Use a rasp to do a little preliminary tidying of the fresh-cut edges of the wood roll, then clamp the visible leaf against the fence on your drill press and cut the hole into which you will later fit the hinge pin. Shown here is a fence I use in my chairmaking shop. Yours doesn't need to be so large. All you need are two boards tacked together at a 90° angle.

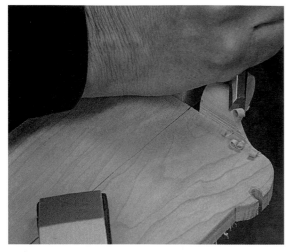

step 13 After band-sawing the contour of the visible leaf, refine — with a paring chisel — the fresh-cut edges of the wood roll. Do this carefully to avoid breaking out these fragile edges.

step 14 With a pencil, mark the bevels around the band-sawn contour of the visible leaf. These lines, which are drawn freehand, mark the limits of the bevel on the top and edges of the visible leaf. Don't fuss too much with the marking. You're going to refine these lines with chisels, gouges, rasps and sandpaper.

step 15 Use carving chisels and a mallet to rough in the bevels. To cut bevels on concave shapes, use a gouge with a smaller radius than the radius of the concave shape.

step 16 With a paring chisel, create the long, straight bevels on either side of the visible leaf. Pay attention to grain direction when paring these long bevels. If the grain is diving down into the work in the direction in which you're paring, the chisel will tear out chunks of material. Instead, you should work in the direction of rising grain.

step 17 Clean up the carved bevels with rasps and sandpaper. When working on the tightest concave bevels, make a custom-fit rasp by rolling a bit of cloth-backed 80-grit sandpaper into a shape that fits into those tight spots.

step 18 After planing a piece of cherry to a thickness that fits snugly into the hinge-key notch, mark the hole for the hinge pin. The edge of the hinge-key stock — into which the hinge-pin hole will be drilled — should be pressed tight into the notch.

step 19 With a temporary hinge pin holding the key material into place, mark the outside contour of the hinge key. Notice the tri-square, which keeps the leaf perpendicular to the key during the marking process.

step 21 After assembling the hidden-leaf frame with fat dovetails, sketch its outside shape. (See chapter ten for cutting dovetails by hand.)

step 20 After band-sawing the key's profile, glue the hinge pin into place. Only the two ends of the hinge pin should be glued. The center section of the hinge pin's length must remain unglued to allow the pin to rotate in the hole when the leaf is raised. Once the pin is glued into place, do the final shaping of the key profile.

step 22 Then, on the band saw, cut the outside profile of the hidden-leaf frame.

step 23 On a router table, using a bit equipped with a pilot bearing, cut the rabbet into which the back of the hidden leaf will fit.

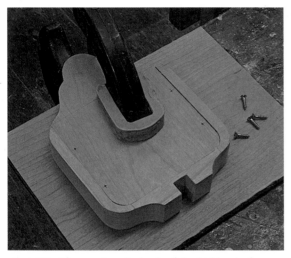

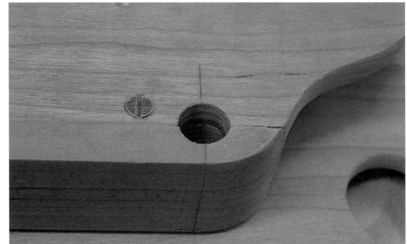

step 24 After cutting the back of the hidden leaf to shape, screw it into place.

step 25 If the visible leaf isn't closed with a catch, its center of gravity will cause it to fall slightly open when hung on a wall. To correct this problem I used a rare earth magnet as a catch. The catch plate (against which the magnet draws) is the head of a short-bodied sheet-metal screw that is fully countersunk on the inside surface of the visible leaf. The mortise into which the magnet is placed must be aligned with the mortises in which the sheet-metal screw will be countersunk. To achieve this alignment, square a line across the back of the hidden leaf, then continue that line on the hidden leaf's outside edge and mark where that line intersects the back surface of the visible leaf. Square a line across the back side of the visible leaf. Both the magnet mortise and the sheet-metal screw mortise will be positioned along these lines.

TIP

Before using a rasp to clean up saw marks on a curved edge, take a bit of coarse sandpaper and relieve the corner on the side of the edge opposite the one facing you. This relief reduces the chances of the rasp catching the end grain of wood fibers on that opposite edge and splintering those fibers away. In this photo, the corner of the edge facing the viewer is the one that has been relieved.

step 26 This is the rare earth magnet in its mortise, and the sheet-metal screw in its mortise. When the key cache is closed, magnetism passes through the ⅛" of wood at the bottom of the magnet mortise and reacts with the metal head of the screw, holding the visible leaf in place.

step 27 To hold the rare earth magnet in place, insert the magnet, then pack the mortise with strips of cloth. Glue a wood plug in place atop the packing. The plug should not be tapped into place, because its tapered shape could split the material into which the mortise is cut. Instead, apply glue to the plug and press it into place with your finger. With a chisel, pare down the glued plug so that it sits flush with the back of the key cache.

Repairing Chipped Wood

1 While shaping the bevel with a gouge I broke off a chip of wood. Fortunately, such a piece can be easily glued and reattached.

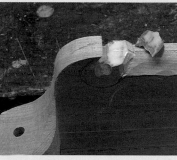

2 I thoroughly glued both split edges.

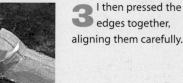

3 I then pressed the edges together, aligning them carefully.

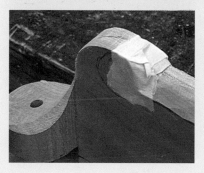

4 Because no clamp could hold such a tiny chip without crushing it, I held it in place with a few strips of masking tape. In an hour I removed the tape and went back to work.

band-sawn maple
change box

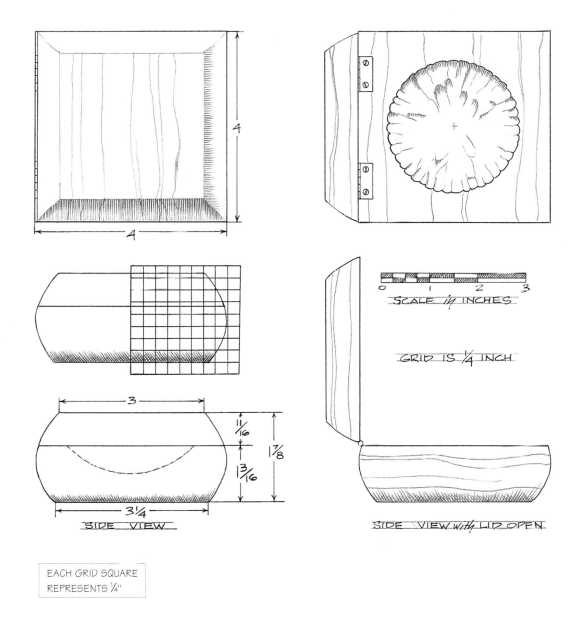

4

4

SCALE IN INCHES

GRID IS ¼ INCH

3

¹¹⁄₁₆

1⅞

1³⁄₁₆

3¼

SIDE VIEW

SIDE VIEW with LID OPEN

EACH GRID SQUARE
REPRESENTS ¼"

The splitting and excavating technique employed in the construction of this box can be used to create enclosures from scrap of virtually any size. With a larger set of hinges, the technique could be used to create a humidor. With a single hinge of the smallest available size, the technique could be used to produce a nest for one piece of jewelry.

materials list
band-sawn maple change box

inches

REFERENCE	QTY.	DIMENSIONS T W L
Box	1 pc.	2 x 4 x 4
Hinges	2 pcs.	1/2 x 3/4

millimeters

REFERENCE	QTY.	DIMENSIONS T W L
Box	1 pc.	51 x 102 x 102
Hinges	2 pcs.	13 x 19

step 1 This cutoff has a number of defects, the most obvious of which is a big knot and a lot of swirling grain surrounding it.

step 2 Cut off the most promising section of your scrap and run it through your planer so that you can make a more informed decision about what part would be best for this project.

step 3 Here, too, are some problems. Notice the unsightly brown flecks. Unfortunately, these are common in maple.

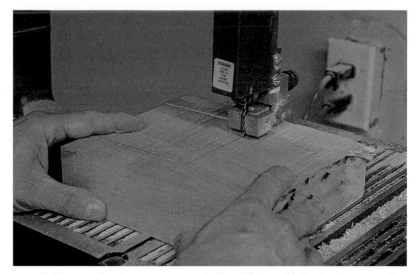

step 4 Once you've looked over the piece carefully, front and back, lay out the section from which the box will be made, taking care to avoid material marred by any defects.

step 5 Use your band saw to cut out the box. This could also be done on a jigsaw or even using a handheld jigsaw. However, if — like me — you're working with a wood as dense as hard maple, you may be asking more of your tool than it can supply.

step 6 Make a pattern of the box's outside profile from a bit of scrap. Then transfer that profile to one of the box's two end-grain sides using a pencil. Marking on the end-grain sides is important because the material you cut away must remain intact so that it can be taped back into place after cutting. If you marked first on one of the box's long-grain sides, you would be cutting away material that would break apart as you tried to tape it back into place.

step 7 Carefully cut away the scrap. Be sure to keep the bottom side of the box resting solidly on the band saw table. If you jiggle the box during this process, the band saw cuts will not be perpendicular to the band saw table and, therefore, to the bottom side of the box.

step 8 Tape the scraps cut from one side of the box back into place. The two pieces of scrap must be positioned so that the uncut wood in the center of the box side, and the flat surfaces of the scrap, form a single plane.

step 9 Use a tri-square to verify that the plane you created by taping the scrap into place is perpendicular to the bottom of the box.

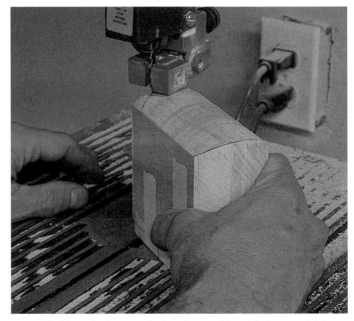

step 10 Use the profile pattern to mark the box's two remaining sides. The pencil line in this photo appears to diverge from the pattern because the sides being marked have already been profiled.

step 11 Place the box on the band saw table with the taped side on the bottom. Then cut the profiles of the box's two remaining sides.

step 12 With a block plane, true up the profiles on all four sides of the box. Even the end-grain sides can be shaped in this way, although it's necessary to work the end-grain sides from the left and right toward the middle. This prevents breakout material at the end of the plane stroke.

step 13 Make frequent visual checks of the profiles as you plane.

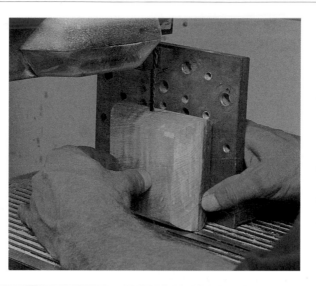

step 14 I used a Craftsman universal table saw jig to cut away the lid. This jig rides on a bar that fits into the band saw's miter-gauge slot. The upright face of the jig is adjustable to permit the creation of box lids of various thicknesses. A nonadjustable shop-built jig capable of this task could be assembled from a few scraps.

step 15 Remove the band saw marks from the bottom of the lid with a wide butt chisel used as a scraper. Place the tip of the butt chisel, bevel side away from you, on the work. Draw the chisel toward you with one hand while applying downward pressure on the chisel with the other hand. If the chisel is properly sharpened, this action will produce shavings and the band saw marks will quickly disappear.

step 16 Perform the same operation on the top face of the bottom of the box.

step 17 Although the scraping will quickly remove band saw marks, it may leave the cut surfaces with some areas higher than others. To remedy this, place a sheet of 100-grit sandpaper on your bench top and rub the cut surfaces until they are level.

step 18 When you position the box lid onto the bottom of the box, you will notice that the two halves don't mate up quite right. This is because of the material removed during the cutting and smoothing operations.

step 19 Tape the box together as shown, then fair the two untaped surfaces with a rasp. Remove the tape, retape the box in the opposite direction and fair the remaining surfaces.

step 20 Mark the hinge locations with a sharp knife. Then cut the hinge mortises with a paring chisel. These hinges and their mortises are quite small, so any sloppiness in the mortises is noticeable. It's important, therefore, to proceed cautiously.

step 21 Once the hinges have been installed in the bottom of the box, place the top of the box into position and mark the locations of the hinges on the top of the box. Then remove the hinges from the bottom of the box, place them on the top of the box in the marked locations, and mark the perimeters of the hinges with your knife. After cutting the mortises in the top of the box, install the hinges on both the top and bottom of the box.

step 22 Unless your mortises are perfectly located — unlike mine — it's necessary to do a little fairing with a rasp so that the top and the bottom of the box align perfectly.

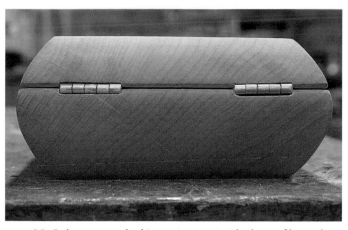

step 23 I chose to set the hinge pins just inside the profile on the back of the box in order to keep a clean line. It was necessary, therefore, to bevel the back edges of the box. Without these bevels, the box couldn't be opened fully.

step 24 Remove the hinges and locate the center of the box bottom by crossing the diagonals. With a compass, draw the perimeter of the excavation.

step 25 With a No. 5 sweep gouge, begin clearing out the waste.

step 26 Finalize the excavation with a No. 8 sweep gouge.

step 27 I chose to keep the tool marks inside the excavation because I like the contrast between that texture and the smooth texture of the outside of the box.

two honey dippers

When you slide a honey dipper into an open jar of honey the syrup collects in the grooves. Then, when the dipper is moved to a slice of toast or a biscuit, the honey oozes from the grooves. Maybe this method of honey conveyance isn't very practical, but I think the turned wooden dippers create a more elegant appearance on your kitchen counter than a plastic squeeze bottle shaped like a bear.

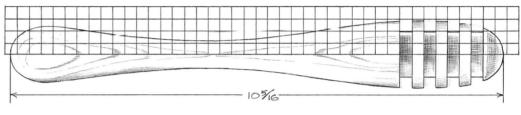

10⁵⁄₁₆

0   1   2   3
SCALE IN INCHES

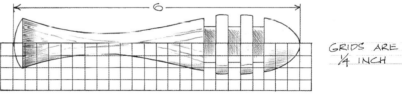

6

GRIDS ARE
¼ INCH

EACH GRID SQUARE
REPRESENTS ¼"

materials list
two honey dippers

inches

REFERENCE	QTY.	DIMENSIONS T W L
Small dipper	1 pc.	$1\frac{1}{4} \times 1\frac{1}{4} \times 6$
Large dipper	1 pc.	$1\frac{3}{8} \times 1\frac{3}{8} \times 10\frac{5}{16}$

millimeters

REFERENCE	QTY.	DIMENSIONS T W L
Small dipper	1 pc.	32 x 32 x 152
Large dipper	1 pc.	35 x 35 x 262

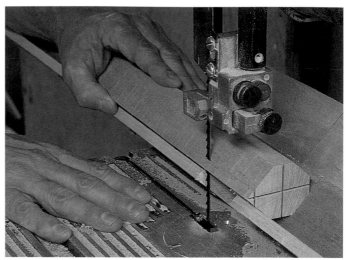

step 1 Place one corner of your square turning stock in the notch in front of your band saw blade. This notch, visible in step two, runs from the front of the table to the blade. Hold the stock so the opposite corner of the stock aligns with the blade. Press the stock gently against the blade. Rotate the stock 90° and repeat. On the end grain of your stock, you've identified the centers and you've created notches for the spurs on your lathe's drive center.

step 2 I use this jig to cut off the corners on chair-post stock. Removing these corners makes the rough-turning process much less stressful.

step 4 Use a parting tool to mark the ends of the honey dipper. You need to go deep enough so that you can shape the ends of the dipper but not so deep that you weaken the spindle. I left about ⅝" of stock at the bottom of the parting-tool cut.

step 3 With your roughing gouge, reduce the octagonal turning blank to a cylinder.

TIP I'm left handed. If you're right handed, you will feel more comfortable holding your tools in your right hand.

step 5 With a ½" or ¾" fingernail gouge, rough in the middle of the dipper.

step 6 Place your skew on your tool rest with the point down and the skew resting on one corner at a 45° angle to the tool rest. Then bring the skew into the work so that the point meets the work ⅛" from the end of the cut made by the parting tool. Rotate the skew into the parting-tool cut so that the point peels material away creating a radius on the end of the dipper. This should be done in several passes, each one beginning ⅛" farther back from the parting-tool cut, continuing until the desired radius has been achieved.

step 7 Because the spindle is beginning to get long and thin, it will chatter (vibrate against the tool, leaving behind unsightly marks) if it is unsupported. I support the back side of the work with a pad made of masking tape held in my off hand (the one not holding the tool).

step 8 Supporting the work with your off hand, further refine the shape in the middle of the dipper.

step 9 With a rule, lay out the grooves you're going to cut in the head of the honey dipper. These should be made so that each is a bit wider than the tip of your parting tool.

step 10 Cut each of the grooves holding a set of calipers set to the correct size in your off hand and your parting tool in your strong hand. When the calipers slip onto the work, you know you have reached the correct size.

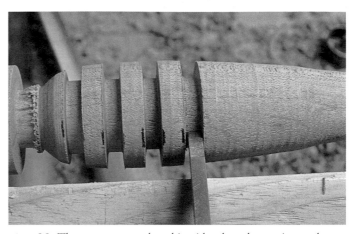

step 11 The grooves must be a bit wider than the parting tool, otherwise the tool will begin to burn the wood from friction with the sidewalls of the groove. Work the tool across the full width of the groove as you approach the final depth of cut.

step 12 Sand with a variety of grits. My sequence is 80 grit first, if necessary, 100 grit, 150 grit, then 220 grit.

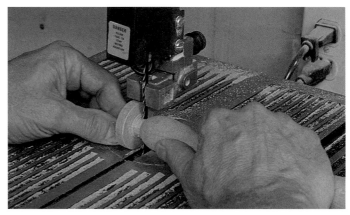

step 13 Cut off the ends of your dipper on your band saw.

step 14 Shape the ends with a paring chisel.

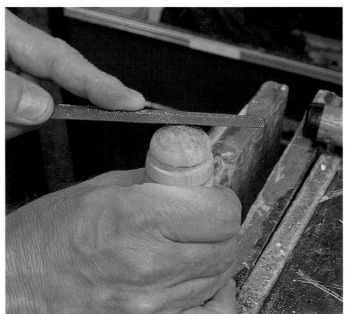

step 15 Finish with a rasp and sandpaper.

cherry spoon

materials list
cherry spoon

inches

QUANTITY	DIMENSIONS T W L
1 pc.	1¼ x 2⅜ x 8¾

millimeters

QUANTITY	DIMENSIONS T W L
1 pc.	32 x 61 x 222

Here's a project that can be made in a couple of hours from a scrap of almost any size, shape or species. Simply apply the two primary techniques — creating the basic form by band-sawing in two adjacent planes and excavating the spoon bowl with carving gouges — to whatever scrap you have in your shop.

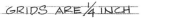

GRIDS ARE ¼ INCH   SIDE VIEW

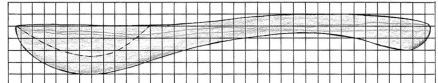

2⅜   TOP VIEW

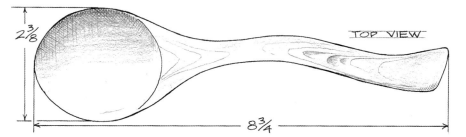

8¾

BOTTOM VIEW

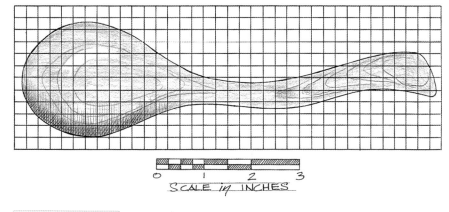

0   1   2   3
SCALE IN INCHES

EACH GRID SQUARE
REPRESENTS ¼"

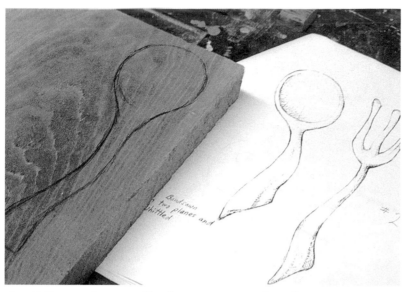

step 2 Cut out that profile on your band saw.

step 1 Lay out the top profile of your spoon on a piece of scrap.

step 3 Then sketch in the side profile on an adjacent plane.

step 4 Cut out that side profile on your band saw.

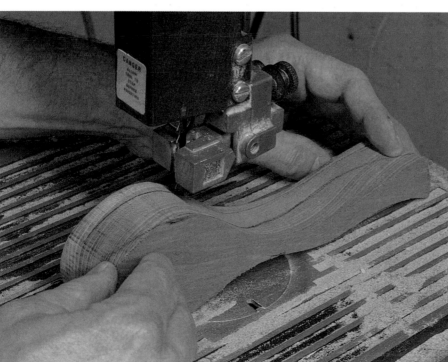

step 5 Clamp the spoon blank to your bench top and begin removing waste from the spoon bowl with a carving gouge. I used a No. 8 sweep.

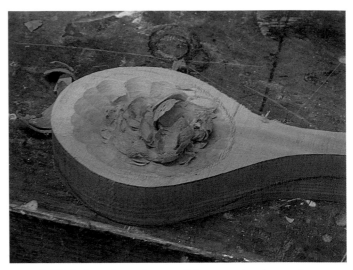

step 6 Work from the perimeter of the spoon bowl toward the center.

step 7 Once the bowl has been roughed in, clamp the spoon blank facedown on your bench and begin creating the outside surface of your spoon bowl. I used a No. 5 sweep.

step 8 Move the clamp position from time to time in order to gain access to the full length of the spoon blank.

step 9 Your bench vise also makes a good holding tool for this irregularly shaped blank.

step 10 Once the spoon handle has been roughed in with carving gouges, use a rasp to fair the surfaces. If you're working with a relatively fragile wood, like cherry, support the handle throughout the rasping process.

step 11 You may find it easier to hold the blank in your lap when you fair the outside surface of the bowl.

step12 Make regular visual checks of the shapes you're creating.

step 13 I used a No. 5 carving gouge to create the shapes at the very end of the spoon handle.

step 14 Use a piece of 80-grit sandpaper to fair the inside of the bowl.

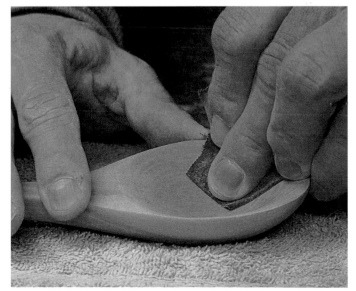

step 15 Sand thoroughly through a number of grits, finishing with 320.

ash comb

I made the first edition of this comb from a beautiful piece of figured maple. The teeth, however, were too fragile so I reluctantly set it aside and opted then for ash. Although this material doesn't have the beauty of figured maple, it does produce a comb with teeth that are almost impossible to break. The unusual finish on this piece was achieved in an unorthodox manner. I began by applying a coat of blue craft paint, which I then stripped off. The result — as you can see at the left — is a deposit of pigment in all the fissures in this coarse-grained material.

GRID IS ¼ INCH

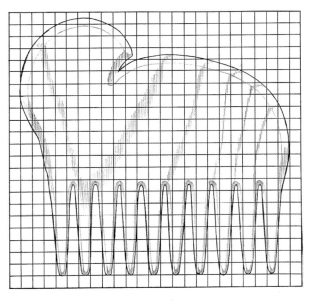

EACH GRID SQUARE
REPRESENTS ¼"

SCALE in INCHES
0 1 2 3

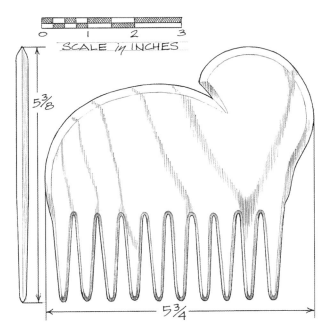

5⅜

5¾

materials list
ash comb

inches

QUANTITY	DIMENSIONS T W L
1 pc.	$\frac{1}{4}$ x $5\frac{3}{8}$ x $5\frac{3}{4}$

millimeters

QUANTITY	DIMENSIONS T W L
1 pc.	6 x 137 x 146

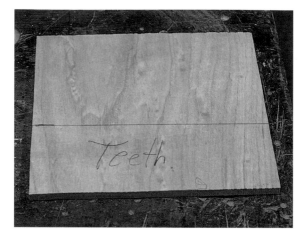

step 1 Plane the stock to $\frac{1}{4}$" thickness. Sketch in a line marking the separation between the teeth and the spine of the comb.

step 2 Clamp the stock securely to your bench top. Then, with a jack plane (or a block plane) create a taper extending from the line to what will later be the tip of the comb's teeth. Repeat on the reverse side of the comb stock.

step 3 The taper can be seen in this end view of the comb stock.

step 4 Sketch in the shape of the comb.

step 5 Cut the profile of the comb on your band saw or jigsaw.

step 6 Sit down in a comfortable chair and begin refining the shape of each tooth with a knife. Some cuts will be most easily made with the knife cutting away from you.

step 7 Some cuts will be easier with the knife cutting toward you.

step 8 Cut a rounded bevel on the edges of the comb's spine with a wide sweep carving gouge. Finish with rasps and sandpaper.

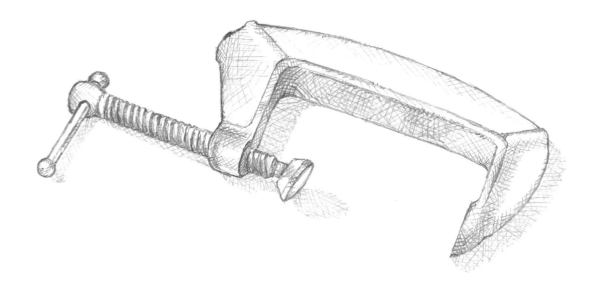

mixed-wood cutting board

Because this project uses a number of different pieces of scrap, you can finally clean out some of those table saw rips you've accumulated. All you need is material long enough and wide enough to produce the strips from which the cutting board will be assembled. And if your rips don't quite meet the dimensions of those used here, simply reduce the dimensions of your rips to match the size of the smallest in your collection.

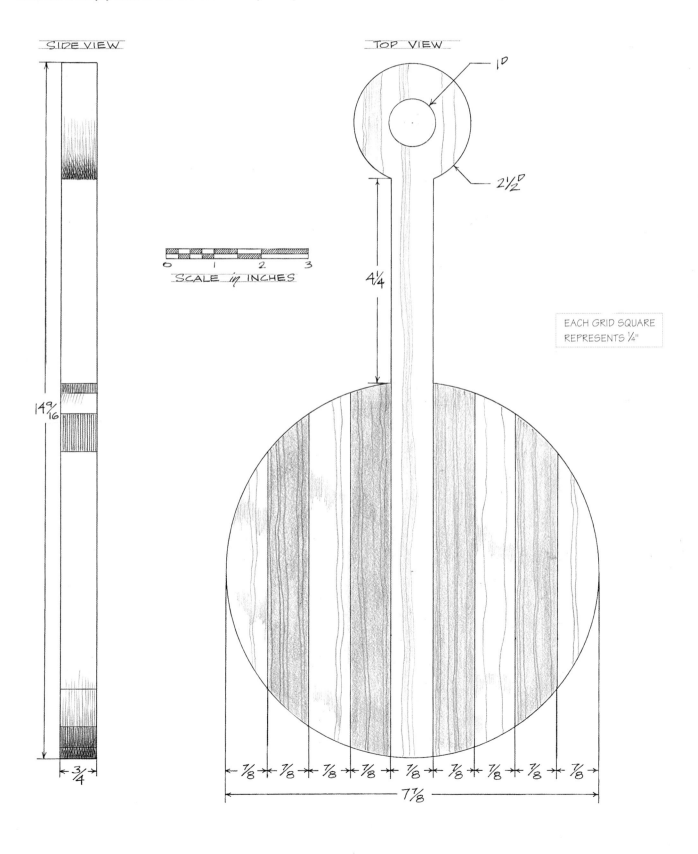

SIDE VIEW

TOP VIEW

1⌀

2½⌀

4¼

14⁹⁄₁₆

¾

EACH GRID SQUARE
REPRESENTS ¼"

SCALE in INCHES

⅞ ⅞ ⅞ ⅞ ⅞ ⅞ ⅞ ⅞ ⅞

7⅞

materials list
mixed-wood cutting board

inches

ITEM	QUANTITY	DIMENSIONS T W L
Center piece	1 pc.	$3/4 \times 2^{1/2} \times 14^{9/16}$
Second pieces	2 pcs.	$3/4 \times 7/8 \times 7^{7/8}$
Third pieces	2 pcs.	$3/4 \times 7/8 \times 7^{7/16}$
Fourth pieces	2 pcs.	$3/4 \times 7/8 \times 6^{9/16}$
Fifth pieces	2 pcs.	$3/4 \times 7/8 \times 4^{15/16}$

millimeters

ITEM	QUANTITY	DIMENSIONS T W L
Center piece	1 pc.	19 x 64 x 370
Second pieces	2 pcs.	19 x 22 x 200
Third pieces	2 pcs.	19 x 22 x 189
Fourth pieces	2 pcs.	19 x 22 x 166
Fifth pieces	2 pcs.	19 x 22 x 126

step 1 Select the scraps and cutoffs you intend to use.

step 2 Rip your strips. Run them through the planer to see the quality of your stock. Check color and figure by brushing the stock with mineral spirits. I left the cherry rip its full width. Although I hadn't finalized the design of the cutting board, I'd already decided to cut the eye from which the cutting board would hang.

step 3 With a compass, draw the profile of the eye.

step 4 Create a center line for the cherry strip by aligning a straightedge with the compass point in the center of the eye. Measure out in both directions from that center line a distance half the width of the ripped strips that will surround this center strip.

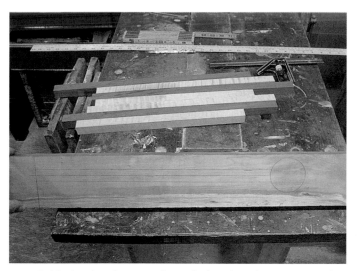

step 5 Notice that the eye and attached rip have been positioned to avoid the many defects on this piece of cherry.

step 6 Cut out this center strip on the band saw.

step 7 Because of the eye, the center strip can't be edge-jointed on a jointer like the other rips. Create the glue joints with a block plane, working as close to the eye as possible. Then finish the last couple of inches with a scraper or rasp.

step 8 Remove band saw marks from the eye with a rasp and sandpaper.

step 9 Experiment with several different arrangements of strips until you find one that pleases your eye. I ultimately decided that I would confine myself to three species: cherry, walnut and curly maple.

step 10 Using a Forstner bit in your drill press, cut the hole in the center of the eye.

step 11 Before gluing up the stock, position the strips. Then use your compass to sketch the approximate location of the circle you will eventually cut. These lines are important because they will tell you how to position the stock when it's glued and placed within the clamp.

step 12 Before gluing up any assembly, lay out your tools and materials, then work your way through a dry clamping. This is important because it allows you to solve any problems that might arise during the gluing-up process, before the glue is on the wood and you're hurrying to get everything positioned and clamped.

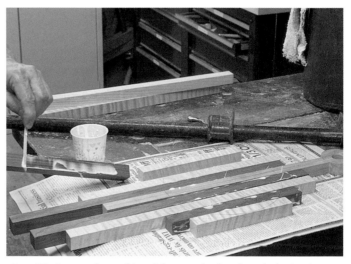

step 13 I use a short, thin stick to apply the glue, slathering it pretty generously on both sides that are to be joined.

step 14 Draw the clamped parts together using as much force as you can apply to the clamp screw. Then wash away the squeeze-out with a damp rag.

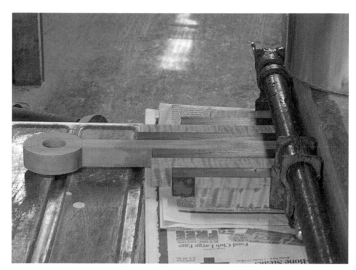

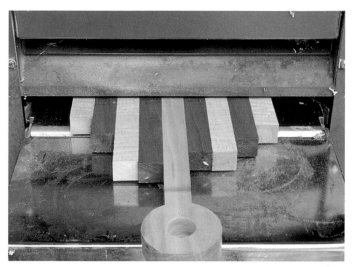

step 15 Clamp together the assembly and set it aside to dry. It should dry overnight before you do any machining. I used a short 4×4 and a can of roof cement to keep the assembly flat during the curing process.

step 16 The next day, remove the clamps and run the assembly through your thickness planer (this can also be done the old-fashioned way: with a jack plane) to even out the top and bottom surfaces of the rips from which it's constructed.

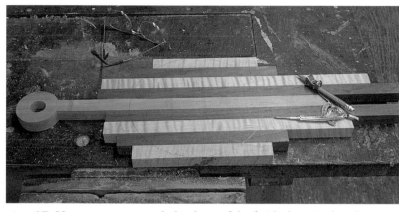

step 17 Use a compass to mark the shape of the finished cutting board.

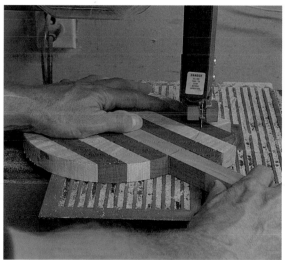

step 18 Cut the profile on the band saw.

step 19 Before rasping away the band saw marks from the end grain at the top and bottom of the cutting board body, create a bevel on the back side of the edge you're working, like the one shown here. This bevel will keep the rasp from breaking out the grain on the back side.

basket for cut flowers

This basket can be made from just two pieces of wood: one a section of $\frac{1}{4}$" material 7" wide and 14" long, and the

other a $\frac{3}{16}$" rip 1$\frac{1}{4}$" wide and 45" long. I used an ash rip for the handle because ash bends very nicely, but white

oak could also be used here, and virtually any wood could be used for the dovetailed body of the basket.

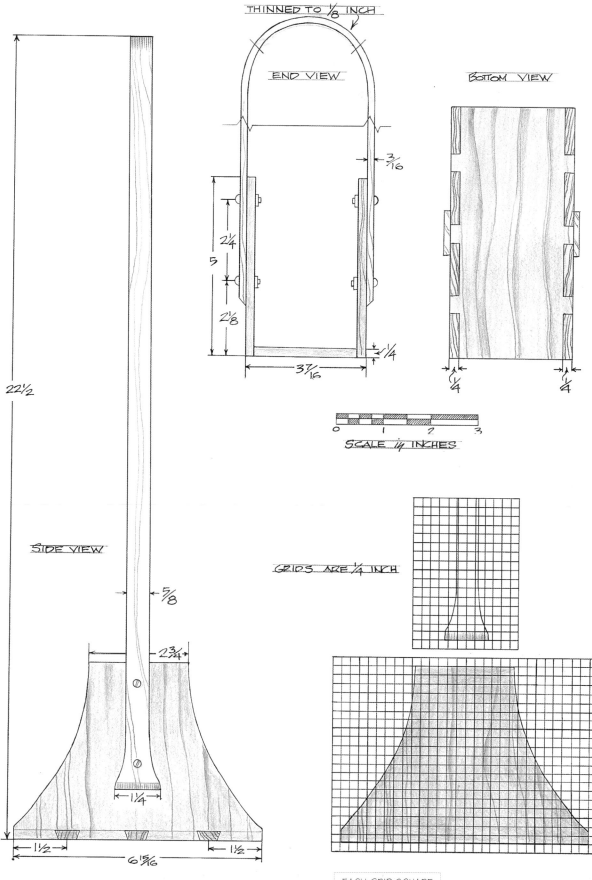

THINNED TO ⅛ INCH

END VIEW

BOTTOM VIEW

3/16

2¼

5

2⅛

3 7/16

¼

¼   ¼

SCALE IN INCHES

22½

SIDE VIEW

GRIDS ARE ¼ INCH

5/8

2¾

1¼

1½

6 15/16

1½

EACH GRID SQUARE
REPRESENTS ¼"

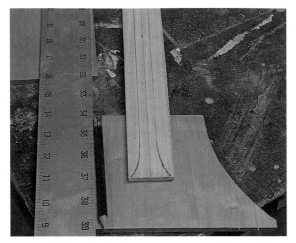

step 1 Although the photos are presented in a single sequence with the handle being built first, I actually worked on the handle and body simultaneously. The photo above shows the shape relationship I tried to achieve between the profile of the basket body and the profiles at the ends of the handle.

step 2 After planing and cutting out the band-sawn profiles of the handle, the edges must be dressed. However, the profiles at the ends of the handle won't allow these edges to be passed over the jointer. To dress these long edges, clamp the handle between two pieces of wood in your vise so the band-sawn edge peeks up over the pieces of wood. Then work this edge with a block plane.

step 3 The very ends of the handle should be worked with a rasp.

materials list
basket for cut flowers

inches

ITEM	QUANTITY	DIMENSIONS T W L
Sides	2 pcs.	$^1/_4$ x 5 x 6$^{15}/_{16}$
Bottom	1 pc.	$^1/_4$ x 3$^7/_{16}$ x 6$^{15}/_{16}$
Handle	1 pc.	$^3/_{16}$ x 1$^1/_4$ x 44$^1/_8$
Brass machine screws and nuts	4 pcs.	$^1/_8$ x $^3/_4$

Note: Allow an extra $^1/_{32}$" of length to dovetailed parts so you can clean up end-grain saw marks.

millimeters

ITEM	QUANTITY	DIMENSIONS T W L
Sides	2 pcs.	6 x 127 x 176
Bottom	1 pc.	6 x 87 x 176
Handle	1 pc.	5 x 32 x 1121
Brass machine screws and nuts	4 pcs.	3 x 19

Note: Allow an extra 1mm of length to dovetailed parts so you can clean up end-grain saw marks.

step 4 Cut a bevel on the end of the handle with a paring chisel.

step 5 The pencil mark on the edge of the handle marks the halfway point along the handle's length. Scrape away $\frac{1}{16}$" of thickness 4" each way from that halfway point. This is the section of the handle that will be bent. The extra thinness makes the bend easier to create.

step 6 My steamer cost me $15. I heat water in a garage-sale deep-fat fryer to generate steam, which is then conducted, through an opening cut in the fryer's lid, into a length of PVC. The ladder is simply there to stabilize this awkward construction. Although it looks pretty crude, I've successfully steamed the slats and back posts for hundreds of post-and-rung chairs in this device.

step 7 This close-up of the top of the steamer with the lid cocked open shows the steady flow of steam that is conducted over any part inside the section of PVC.

step 8 After you've steamed the handle, take it immediately to the bending form and fix it into place. The form, which you'll prepare in advance, is just a length of scrap band-sawn to the bend of the finished handle.

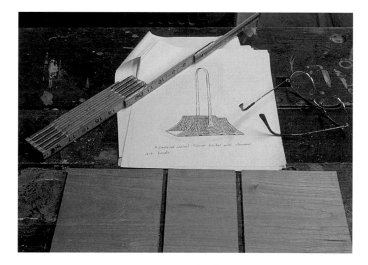

step 9 The body of the basket can be made from a single piece of wood cut into three sections, or it could be made from three different pieces of wood.

step 10 Trace the curve onto one of the end pieces. After cutting the curve, use it as a guide to mark the others.

step 11 Before you begin to cut a set of dovetails by hand, you need to establish depth lines across the width of all the parts to be dovetailed. These lines should be scored with a knife, rather than drawn with a pencil, because knife scorings later give you positive locations in which you can register the tip of your chisel when you're paring down to the mark. In this case, I set the marks a bit less than $5/16$" from the end of the piece. That allows the pins and tails to protrude a bit more than the $1/4$" thickness of the parts. Most woodworkers use a marking gauge for this task, but since I don't have one I just measure and score.

step 12 Lay out the tails on the bottoms of the two end pieces. Sketch the approximate angles you'll be cutting, but don't worry if the angle you cut is a little different from the one you've drawn; no one will know. The scribbles identify the waste between the tails. Because the material is very thin, you can use your fine-toothed backsaw to cut the tails in both end pieces at the same time.

step 13 With a coping saw, remove the bulk of the waste between the tails. Don't worry about precision. You'll clean the bottoms of each cut with your paring chisel.

step 14 Locate the tip of your paring chisel in the knife scoring and begin to remove the waste. Work at this gradually in several passes. The first pass should be at an oblique angle. Each successive pass should come closer and closer to the perpendicular.

step 15 Before you cut all the way to the perpendicular on one side, flip the end panel over and begin to pare from the back. Your cuts should meet in approximately the middle of the end's thickness.

step 17 Reposition the bottom panel so it sticks up a couple of inches from the top of the vise. Then with a tri-square connect the ends of the lines you just made on the end grain with the scored line on the bottom of the bottom panel.

step 16 Place the bottom panel in your vise so that one end-grain edge just peeks up above the surface of the bench top. Then place the fresh-cut tails onto this end grain. The tails should be aligned so that the knife scoring on the bottom side just meets the bench-side edge of the bottom panel. With a sharp pencil point, mark the pins (those parts of a dovetail joint that fit between the tails) on the end-grain surface of the bottom panel.

step 18 This photo shows the relationship between the pins you've just marked and the tails from which you marked them. Again, the scribbles indicate waste.

step 19 Use your fine-toothed backsaw to cut the sides of each pin. Be sure to keep your saw on the *waste* side of each line.

Fixing Gaps with Cherry Dust

1 Unfortunately, once I had filed away the protruding ends of the pins I saw gaps at two locations above the pins. To remedy this, I created a little cherry dust by running a belt sander over a piece of cherry clamped to my bench.

2 I mixed a thick paste of cherry dust and glue which I then worked into place in those gaps.

step 20 Use a coping saw to hog out the waste between the pins.

step 21 Finalize the waste removal with your paring chisel just as you did when cleaning up the waste between the tails.

step 22 Coat with glue all surfaces that will abut in the finished joint.

step 23 Squeeze the joint together with clamps. It will be necessary to move the clamps back and forth across the width of the basket parts bringing them together gradually. Too much force, too quickly applied at a single location, will bend and then crack one of the end panels.

Take Time to Think About the Work in Progress

This photograph illustrates something I think is often overlooked in the woodshop; taking time to think about the work in progress. At this point in the construction of the basket I'm trying to decide where the handle should be attached. I spring-clamp it into place at several different heights, stepping back each time to assess the placement. It's true that no real work is being done. Nevertheless, I think it's essential that we remember to include this passive activity as part of our woodshop regimen. In some instances, a little time spent thinking can prevent problems from occurring, and when things have taken a bad turn a few minutes of thought can keep us from transforming a simple problem into a disaster. I will also mention that when I looked at this photo several days after taking it, I realized it illustrated another, entirely unrelated, woodshop problem: the complete lack of fashion sense some woodworkers exhibit in their shops. Notice the missing belt and the brown corduroys paired with a gray T-shirt. I'm just glad you can't see the shoes I'm wearing.

step 24 After the glue has cured overnight, use a wood file to bring the protruding ends of the pins level with the surfaces of the tails.

step 25 Use a spring clamp to hold the handle temporarily in place while you drill holes for the bolts that will hold the handle permanently in place. Notice the backup strip I'm holding on the back side of the end panel. This will keep the drill bit from splintering the material when it pierces the back side.

three-tier
keepsake chest

The three tiers of this diminutive chest are all assembled at the same time from the same four pieces of wood. The

tiers are then sawn apart on the table saw. This results in tiers that—in the finished piece—align perfectly.

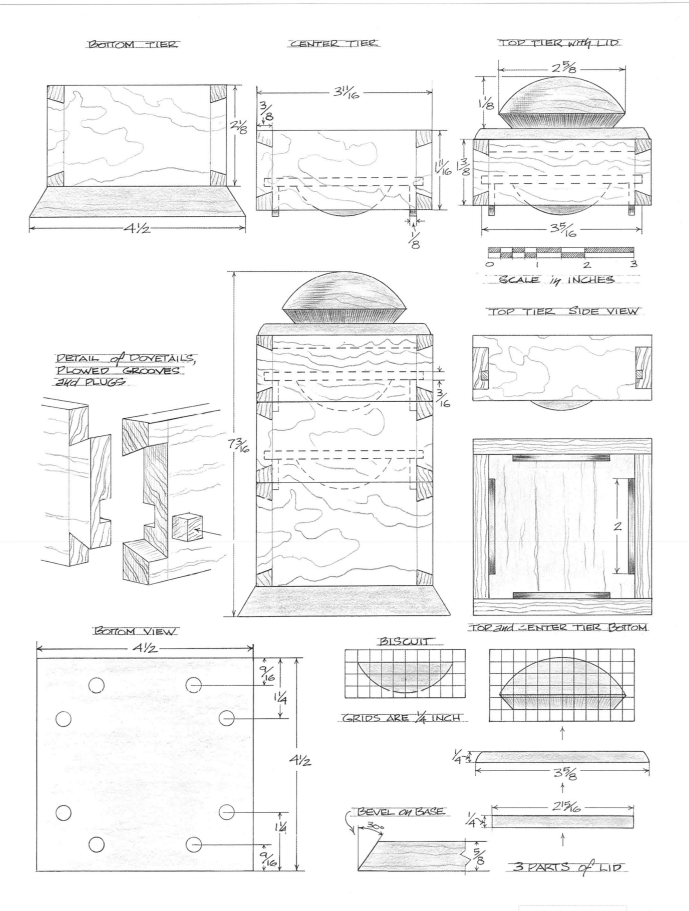

BOTTOM TIER

CENTER TIER

TOP TIER with LID

2 1/8

4 1/2

3 11/16

3/8 8

1 11/16

1/8

2 5/8

1/8

1 3/8

3 5/16

0   1   2   3

SCALE in INCHES

TOP TIER SIDE VIEW

DETAIL of DOVETAILS,
PLOWED GROOVES
and PLUGS

7 3/16

3/16

2

Top and CENTER TIER BOTTOM

BOTTOM VIEW

4 1/2

9/16

1 1/4

4 1/2

1 1/4

9/16

BISCUIT

GRIDS ARE 1/4 INCH

1/4

3 5/8

1/4

2 15/16

BEVEL on BASE

30°

5/8

3 PARTS of LID

EACH GRID SQUARE
REPRESENTS 1/4"

materials list
three-tier keepsake chest

inches

ITEM	QUANTITY	DIMENSIONS T W L
Sides	4 pcs.	$3/8$ x $5^3/_4$* x $3^{11}/_{16}$
Tier bottoms	2 pcs.	$3/16$ x $3^5/_{16}$ x $3^5/_{16}$
Lid bottom	1 pc.	$1/4$ x $3^1/_8$ x $3^1/_8$
Lid top	1 pc.	$1/4$ x $3^5/_8$ x $3^5/_8$
Lid pull	1 pc.	$1^1/_8$ x $2^5/_8$
Dovetail plugs	8 pcs.	$3/16$ x $3/16$ x $3/16$
Base	1 pc.	$5/8$ x $4^1/_2$ x $4^1/_2$
Biscuits	8 pcs.	$1/8$ x $5/8$ x 2
Screws	8 pcs.	#8 x $1^1/_4$"
Brads		

*This includes $9/16$" of width to allow for the box's three tiers to be cut apart.

millimeters

ITEM	QUANTITY	DIMENSIONS T W L
Sides	4 pcs.	10 x 146* x 94
Tier bottoms	2 pcs.	5 x 84 x 84
Lid bottom	1 pc.	6 x 79 x 79
Lid top	1 pc.	6 x 92 x 92
Lid pull	1 pc.	30 x 70
Dovetail plugs	8 pcs.	5 x 5 x 5
Base	1 pc.	16 x 115 x 115
Biscuits	8 pcs.	3 x 16 x 51
Screws	8 pcs.	#8 x 32mm
Brads		

*This includes 14mm of width to allow for the box's three tiers to be cut apart.

step 1 I originally intended to create four tiers, however, when I got into the shop, I realized there simply wasn't enough height for a fourth tier without making significant changes to the chest's proportions. The curly maple and the planed walnut are both cutoffs. The rough-looking walnut was taken from a load of discards.

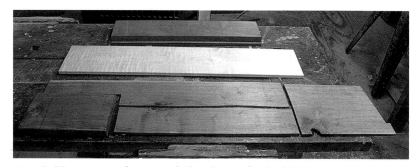

step 2 Here you see the material planed to its finished thicknesses. Notice the sections of the walnut board in the front are planed to three different thicknesses. The thickest piece on the left was cut off once I'd reached the required thickness for the base. I cut out the section closest to the vise once I'd reached the thickness of the tier bottoms. The remainder of this board was planed to the $1/8$" thickness of the tiny arcs that align the tiers.

step 3 Rip to width and cut to length the four sides of the case from which the tiers will be cut. Score lines around each end of the four pieces. These lines should be placed a distance from the ends that is $1/32$" greater than the thickness of the sides; this gives you material to sand away after the chest is assembled in order to remove the end-grain saw marks. Most woodworkers use a marking gauge to create these scorings, but I just mark the distance with a pencil and use a knife to score along the blade of my tri-square.

step 4 This detail shows that scoring, running across the width and the edge of one of the side panels.

step 5 Before you plow the grooves for the tier bottoms, lay out the location of the dovetails and the table saw cuts that will ultimately separate the tiers. The scribbles along the ends of this panel indicate the waste to be removed between the dovetails. (Remember: Only two of the four side panels will have dovetails. The other two panels will have pins that will fit between those dovetails.) The scribbles between the horizontal lines indicate the waste that will be removed when cutting the tiers apart. After you establish these features, locate the grooves to plow on the inside face of each side and end panel.

step 6 Plow the grooves with rabbet cutters on your table saw or a ¼" bit on your router table. The table saw guard has been removed for the purpose of illustration. Never operate a table saw without a blade guard.

step 7 With a fine-tooth backsaw, cut the sides of each dovetail down to the scored line. Remember to keep the saw cut on the *waste* side of the line.

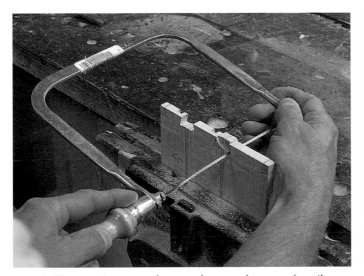

step 8 Use a coping saw to hog out the waste between the tails. Keep the coping saw well above the scored line.

step 9 Rotate the side panel 90° in the vise. Use the backsaw to cut away the waste on one end of the dovetails. Then rotate the panel 180° and cut the waste on the other end.

step 10 Remove the panel from your vise and clamp it to your bench top on a piece of scrap. Then, with a paring chisel, clean up the areas between the dovetails. To do this, locate the tip of the chisel in the scored line and cut an oblique angle. Then on your next pass, make a cut that is closer to the perpendicular.

step 11 Flip the panel over and cut back toward the center from the other side.

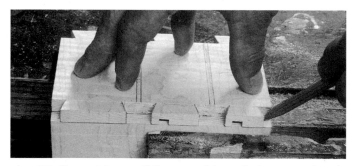

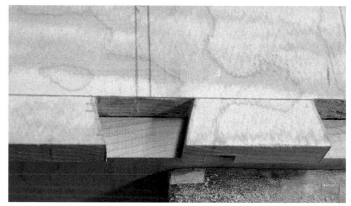

step 12 Once you've cut all four sets of dovetails (one on each end of the two side panels), lay out the first set of pins. Begin by positioning one of the end panels in your vise so the edge just peeks up above the level of the bench top. Place one set of tails on the end-grain edge so the bottom of the waste areas between the tails just meets the inside edge of the end panel. With a sharp pencil, mark the sides of each tail on the end grain of the end panel.

step 13 This detail shows the proper relationship between the dovetail and the pin stock when marking pins.

step 14 Raise the end panel a couple of inches in your vise. Then with your tri-square, connect the marks you just made on the end-grain surface of the end panel with the end panel's scored line. Again, the scribbling indicates waste.

step 15 Cut the sides of each pin with your backsaw. Remember: Your saw cut must be on the *waste* side of the line.

step 16 Use a coping saw to hog out the waste between pins.

step 17 Pare down the waste areas between pins from each side toward the center just as you did when cleaning up between the tails.

step 18 Test fit the tails and pins without fully seating the joint. If you seat the joint fully, you may not be able to get it apart again. Here, the pins and tails fit together without any fine-tuning, but in many cases a little fitting is necessary. Tweak the joint by paring very fine shavings from the sides of the tight pins until a successful fit is accomplished.

step 19 Before gluing up the case, use your block plane to put a slight bevel on all four sides of the tier bottoms to help ease the bottoms into their grooves during assembly.

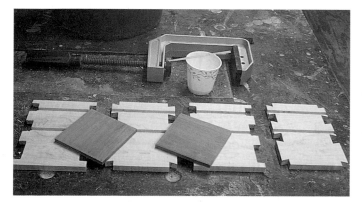

step 20 Before beginning any gluing operation, do a practice run to help you avoid panic situations. Above you can see my preparations for a dry run: all the parts, glue in a paper cup, a glue-spreading stick, the C-clamp to bring the sides together and a bucket of water for cleanup of glue squeeze-out.

step 21 Apply glue to all the areas that will abut in the finished dovetail joint. Then assemble the case around the two bottom panels, which will fit unglued into their grooves.

step 22 Use the C-clamp to squeeze the tails into position between the pins. Do this in increments, working your way up and down the case. Too much pressure too quickly at a single location will crack a side panel.

step 23 After you've washed away any glue squeeze-out, it's time to fill the gaps where the grooves run through the end panels. Plane a length of wood to the same width and thickness as the grooves. Then put a dab of glue on the end of the stick, tap the stick gently into a gap, cut it off and move on to the next gap.

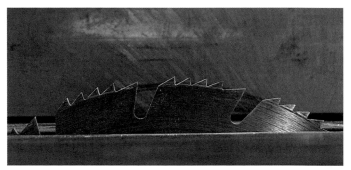

step 24 I dislike the noise and dust generated by a belt sander, but for this particular operation — grinding flush the ends of the pins and tails — it can be persuaded to perform well. If you do use a belt sander, be cautious: This aggressive tool can remove too much material very quickly at a single location. You can substitute a sharp block plane or a rasp, as demonstrated in chapter nine.

step 25 Separate the three tiers by sawing them apart on your table saw. I used a hollow-ground planer blade because it leaves shallower saw marks.

step 26 Carefully push the box past the saw blade. Again, the table saw guard has been removed only for illustration. Never operate a table saw without a blade guard.

step 27 Clean up the saw marks with a block plane.

step 28 When laying out the base allow enough material for the removal of saw marks on the beveled edges.

step 29 With your saw blade set at a 30° angle, rip the base to width.

step 30 Using the miter gauge to guide the stock past the blade, cut the base to width.

step 31 Align the bottom tier on the base. Then mark around that base. These lines will identify the material that must be removed with your block plane in order to establish a good fit.

step 32 Carefully plane the bevels to the correct size.

step 33 Drill the countersunk and through holes for the No. 8 × 1¼" screws you will use to fasten the base to the bottom tier.

step 34 Tape the base to the bottom tier. Then clamp the bottom tier in your vise and attach the base.

step 35 To attach the alignment biscuits, predrill the holes in which you will drive brads.

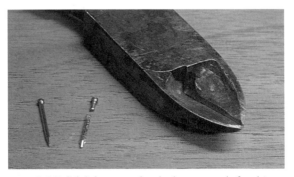

step 36 I didn't have any brads short enough for this particular application, so I snipped ¼" from each with a pair of wire cutters.

step 37 Lay some scrap material into the top tier so that the material reaches to within ³⁄₁₆" of the top of the tier sides.

step 38 Place the lid bottom on top of that scrap material. Notice that the lid bottom completely fills the tier. Notice also that it sticks up ¹⁄₁₆" above the top of the tier sides.

step 39 Slather glue on the top of the lid bottom and bottom of the lid top. Notice that the lid top has been ripped and cut to length at the same 30° angle as the base.

step 41 Attach the lid-pull blank to a piece of scrap with a bit of newspaper in between. I glued up two blanks in case I ran into a problem with the first blank.

step 40 Align these two parts. Then bring them together by clamping them to the top tier.

step 42 Attach the scrap to a faceplate with three screws.

step 43 Turn the faceplate onto the drive center of your lathe.

step 44 With a fingernail gouge, shape the top of the pull.

step 45 With your skew standing on edge, relieve the underside of the pull.

TIP

When you're cutting a set of dovetails, assign a letter to each corner of the case. These letters will help you ensure that you're marking the correct set of pins from the correct set of tails.

step 46 With a paring chisel, separate the pull from the scrap. The bit of newspaper you glued between these two parts will allow a clean separation.

step 47 Scrape away the glue and newspaper from the bottom of the pull.

step 48 Align the pull onto the lid. Glue it in place and clamp.

step 49 Turn a No. 8 × 1¼" wood screw up through three layers of the lid.

set of checkers

materials list
set of checkers

inches

QUANTITY	DIMENSIONS T W L
24 pcs.	$5/16$ x $1^3/8$

millimeters

QUANTITY	DIMENSIONS T W L
24 pcs.	8 x 35

Several times in the last ten years I've considered the possibility of making a set of checkers by slicing each checker from a turned cylinder. What could simpler? The cylinder could be turned in a couple of minutes, and a set of checkers could be sliced off in less time than it takes to describe it. The problem I couldn't solve was this: How could I remove the saw marks from the end-grain surfaces of each checker? It could take me the rest of my natural life to abrade away those marks using hand power, and checkers are much too tiny to be held safely in the fingers and pressed to a machine sander. About halfway through work on this book I came up with what I think is a pretty solid solution.

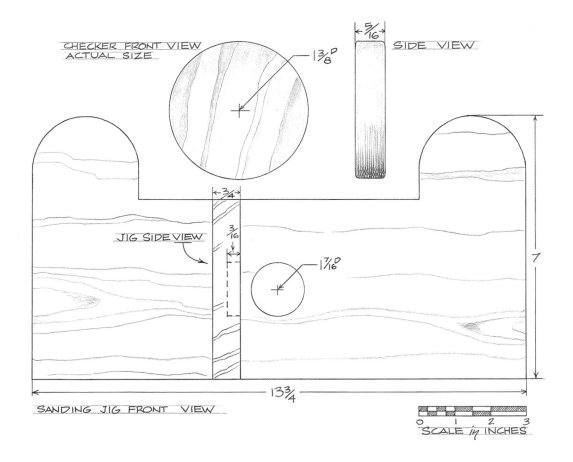

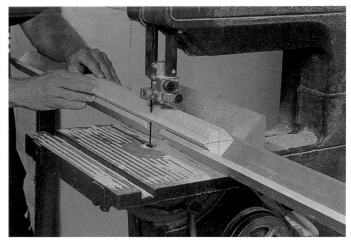

step 1 Cut Xs in the end grain of the cylinder stock you're going to mount in your lathe. The drive spurs on the drive center of your lathe will be pressed into the arms of the Xs when you advance the tail stock. (An easier alternative for cutting this X is shown in chapter five.)

step 2 I built a simple jig to help me change square turning stock into octagonal stock before mounting it in the lathe. Because the octagonal shape approximates a turned cylinder, this step makes the roughing-in of large stock less stressful.

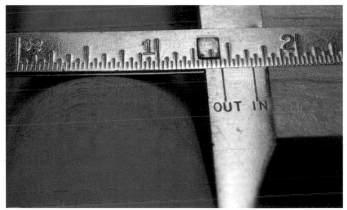

step 4 Put your roughing gouge aside when you've reached the diameter you've selected. I chose 1⁷⁄₁₆".

step 3 With your roughing gouge, round the cylinder.

step 5 Lathe-sand the cylinder through a variety of grits. My sequence is 80 — if necessary — then 100, 150 and 220.

step 7 This view from the top shows the cylinder pressed against the stop block.

step 9 Clamp your belt sander to the top of your workbench, with the body of the sander raised on a piece of scrap so the wheels can turn freely without rubbing the bench top.

TIP I'm left handed. If you're right handed, you will feel more comfortable holding your tools in your right hand.

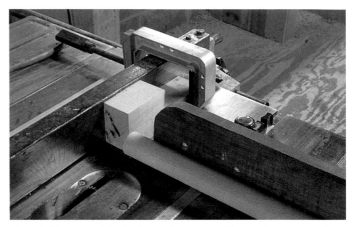

step 6 Use a stop block clamped to your table saw fence to set the thickness of each checker.

step 8 When the miter gauge is moved forward — with the cylinder pressed against it — the blade on your table saw will slice a checker that will have the exact same thickness as every other checker cut in this manner. The blade guard has been removed for the purpose of illustration. Never operate a table saw without a blade guard.

step 10 Make a little jig from a piece of scrap. Exact measurements aren't critical. You just need a few protrusions you can grab with your hands and a hole positioned approximately in the center. The hole should have a slightly greater diameter than the checkers and should be drilled to a depth a bit more than half the thickness of the checker.

step 11 Put a small roll of sticky-side-out tape in the bottom of the hole. This won't hold the checker against the action of the belt sander — the sides of the hole will do that — but the tape will hold the checker in place as you raise the jig and press it against the platen of the belt sander.

step 12 Raise the jig, loaded with a checker, and press it against the platen of the belt sander. Inspect the checker surface frequently to be sure you're achieving a uniformly sanded surface.

step 13 The checker on the lower left has been machine-sanded. The other two checkers have not. Note the saw marks on the other two checkers.

step 14 Finish sanding by rubbing each checker against a sheet of sandpaper laid flat on your bench, using 150, 220, then 320 grit.

porthole picture frames

Large Forstner bits are expensive, but unlike spade bits Forstner bits actually cut round holes. Plus, drilling a large hole with a spade bit can be a tooth-jarring experience as the tremendous torque a spade bit imparts to the workpiece can rip it from your hand (and maybe your arm from your shoulder). True, a large Forstner bit can also impart a fair amount of torque, but in the case of the Forstner bit, most of the energy is invested in cutting the hole — which is exactly where the energy of a drill bit should be invested.

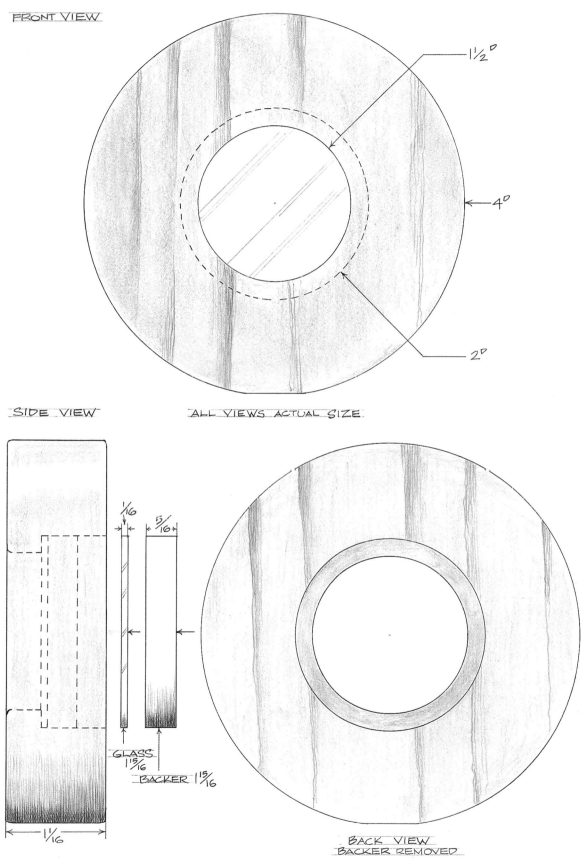

FRONT VIEW

$1\frac{1}{2}''$

$4''$

$2''$

SIDE VIEW　ALL VIEWS ACTUAL SIZE

$\frac{1}{16}$

$\frac{5}{16}$

GLASS
$1\frac{15}{16}$

BACKER $1\frac{15}{16}$

$1\frac{1}{16}$

BACK VIEW
BACKER REMOVED

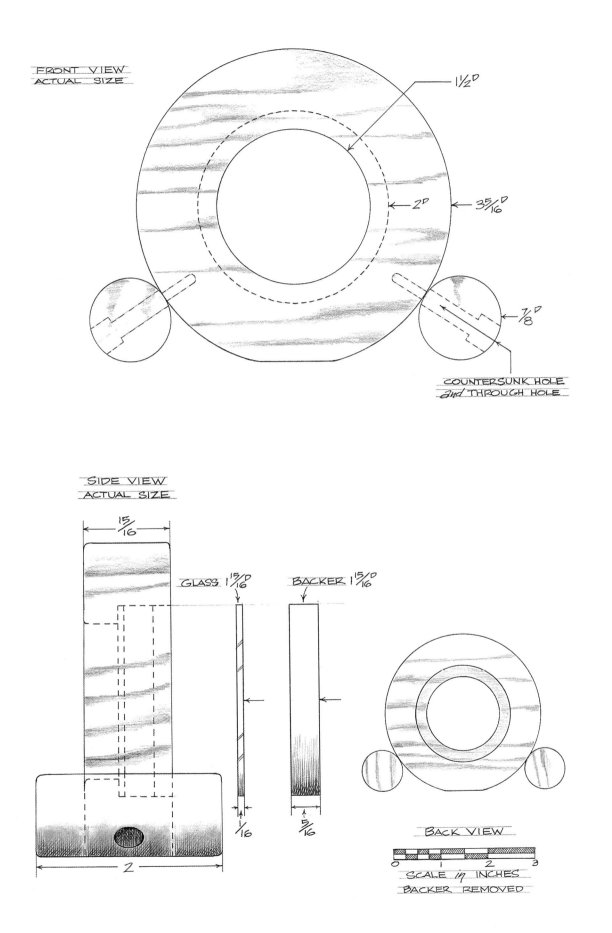

FRONT VIEW
ACTUAL SIZE

$1\frac{1}{2}^{D}$

2^{D}

$3\frac{5}{16}^{D}$

$\frac{7}{8}^{D}$

COUNTERSUNK HOLE
and THROUGH HOLE

SIDE VIEW
ACTUAL SIZE

$\frac{15}{16}$

GLASS $1\frac{15}{16}^{D}$

BACKER $1\frac{15}{16}^{D}$

$\frac{1}{16}$

$\frac{5}{16}$

2

BACK VIEW

0   1   2   3

SCALE in INCHES

BACKER REMOVED

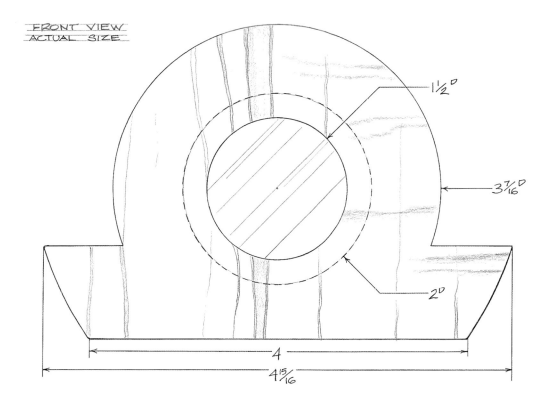

FRONT VIEW
ACTUAL SIZE

$1\frac{1}{2}^{D}$

$3\frac{7}{16}^{D}$

2^{D}

4

$4\frac{15}{16}$

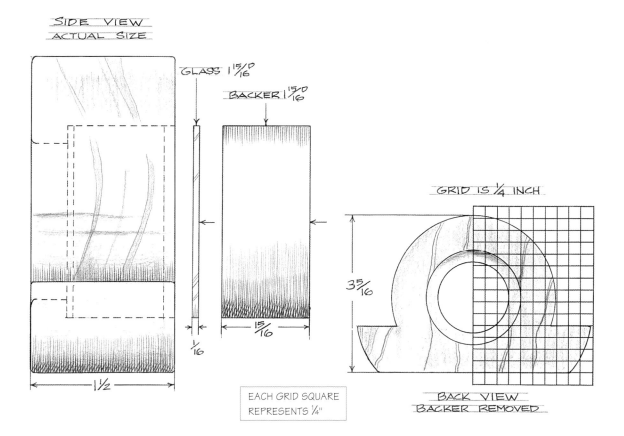

SIDE VIEW
ACTUAL SIZE

GLASS $1\frac{15}{16}^{D}$

BACKER $1\frac{15}{16}^{D}$

$\frac{1}{16}$

$\frac{15}{16}$

$1\frac{1}{2}$

EACH GRID SQUARE
REPRESENTS $\frac{1}{4}$"

GRID IS $\frac{1}{4}$ INCH

$3\frac{5}{16}$

BACK VIEW
BACKER REMOVED

materials list
porthole picture frames

inches

ITEM	QUANTITY	DIMENSIONS T W L
Frame	1 pc.	$1^1/_{16}$ x 4
Glass	1 pc.	$1^1/_{16}$ x $1^{15}/_{16}$
Backer	1 pc.	$5/_{16}$ x $1^{15}/_{16}$
Backer screws	2 pcs.	#4 x $3/_4$"
FRAME WITH TURNED FEET (EACH)		
Frame	1 pc.	$5/_{16}$ x $3^5/_{16}$
Feet	2 pcs.	$7/_8$ x 2
Glass	1 pc.	$1^1/_{16}$ x $1^{15}/_{16}$
Feet screws	2 pcs.	#6 x 1"
Backer screws	2 pcs.	#4 x $3/_4$"
THICK FRAME		
Frame	1 pc.	$1^1/_2$ x $3^{15}/_{16}$ x 4
Backer	1 pc.	$5/_{16}$ x $1^{15}/_{16}$
Backer screws	2 pcs.	#4 x $3/_4$"

millimeters

ITEM	QUANTITY	DIMENSIONS T W L
Frame	1 pc.	26 x 102
Glass	1 pc.	26 x 49
Backer	1 pc.	8 x 49
Backer screws	2 pcs.	#4 x 19mm
FRAME WITH TURNED FEET (EACH)		
Frame	1 pc.	8 x 84
Feet	2 pcs.	22 x 51
Glass	1 pc.	26 x 49
Feet screws	2 pcs.	#6 x 25mm
Backer screws	2 pcs.	#4 x 19mm
THICK FRAME		
Frame	1 pc.	38 x 100 x 102
Backer	1 pc.	8 x 49
Backer screws	2 pcs.	#4 x 19mm

step 1 With your compass, draw several circles with various diameters on some planed scrap. I decided against using the large cherry frame. The image and frame sizes were too disproportionate.

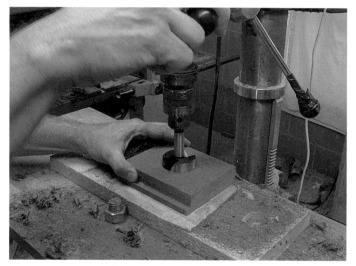

step 2 Use your drill press to create the image size by drilling completely through your stock, centering your $1^1/_2$" Forstner bit in the compass-drawn circle. If you'd rather not use this technique, a holding jig could be quickly cobbled together with a couple of clamps and some scrap lumber.

step 3 Remove the $1^1/_2$" Forstner bit and replace it with your 2" Forstner bit.

step 4 Cut the 2" mortise on the back side of your workpiece, then use this larger bit to excavate the area in which the glass, the picture and the backing board will be housed.

step 5 To save time, I used a drum sander in my drill press to clean up the roughened edges of the hole left by the smaller Forstner bit. The drum sander removes material much more quickly than hand sanding, but it can leave behind a hardened surface that is difficult to work with finer grits.

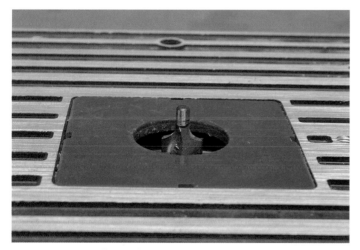

step 6 Use a small roundover bit with a tight radius to break the edges of the smaller hole.

step 7 Once the router bit has been adjusted to the right height, simply place the hole over the bit and run the edges of the hole quickly past the bit. Keep the workpiece moving, because any hesitation that leaves the bit spinning against a stationary workpiece can result in scorched areas.

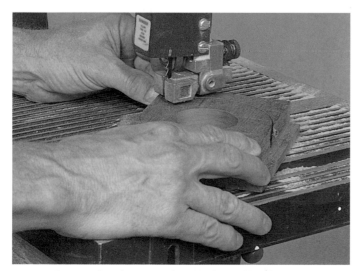

step 8 On your band saw, cut the outside profile of the picture frame.

step 9 Remove the band saw marks on the outside profile with a rasp.

step 10 Run the outside edge of the frame against the router bit as shown here.

step 11 In this photo the frame rests on a flat spot rasped onto the bottom surface.

step 12 Because the two smaller frames are made from thinner stock, they need some additional support. That support will be provided by short cylinders of curly maple that will be screwed to the outside diameter of the frames. If you're turning these cylinders from a figured wood like curly maple, a fair amount of tear-out can occur even when the tool is sharp and the technique good. This can be corrected by planing with a skew — if you are experienced with that technique. If you're not, a few light passes with a fingernail gouge will remove most of the tear-out. The rest can be eliminated with sanding.

step 13 To bore a hole in the center of a cylinder, you need a fence on your drill press. This fence should be set a distance from the lead point of the drill bit that is one-half the diameter of the cylinder. Hold the tiny workpiece in the jaws of a set of channel locks that have been taped to prevent scratching the workpiece. Then bring the drill bit into the work. The first hole will enter the cylinder to a depth of ¼". This hole should be just large enough to accommodate the screw head. The second hole, which is placed in the exact center of the previous hole, should pass completely through the cylinder. This hole should be just large enough to accept the threaded body of the screw.

step 14 See the countersunk hole in the cylinder on the left, and the through-hole in the cylinder on the right.

step 15 If I were a mathematician, I could have calculated the placement of the screw holes on the circumference of the frame, but I don't speak math, so I trial-and-errored my way to the correct placement, conducting my experiments on a scrap disk. I found I needed to center each screw hole $1\frac{19}{32}$" from the center bottom point of the frame. This location gives me three contact points with the surface on which the frames will be placed. Two of those contact points are the bottoms of the cylinders (feet); the third is a slightly flattened area at the bottom center of the frame.

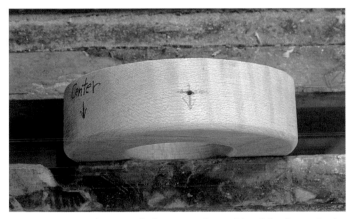

step 16 Locate the screw holes across the width of the frame. Push the tip of an awl into that location to give yourself a place in which to locate the tip of the drill bit. The hole you drill should be small enough to allow the threads on your screws to engage the sides of the hole but large enough to permit the passage of the screw body without splitting the frame. I always drill a sample hole in a bit of scrap to see how well a particular bit is suited to a particular job.

step 17 This photo shows the three contact points at the bottom of the frame.

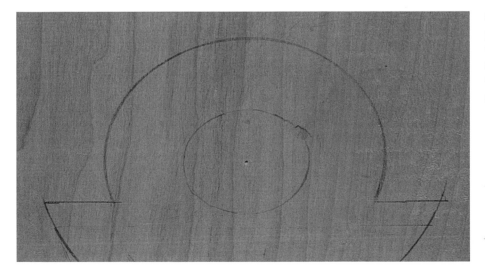

step 18 Create the picture-frame profile by using a compass to draw three concentric circles on your stock. Cut out the frame and use the techniques demonstrated in steps 2-7 to complete it.

desk clock

This project is one of the simplest pieces in this book, but it is also the piece that has most noticeably aroused

the acquisitiveness of my two kids. There's just something cool about handsomely mounted clocks.

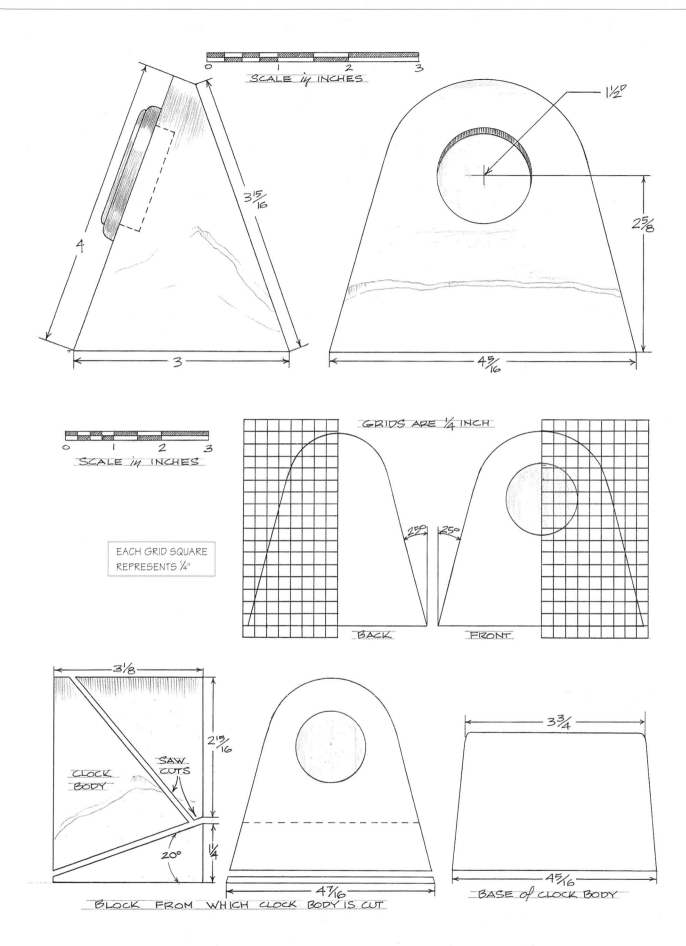

SCALE in INCHES

3 15/16

4

3

1 1/2°

2 5/8

4 5/16

SCALE in INCHES

GRIDS ARE 1/4 INCH

EACH GRID SQUARE
REPRESENTS 1/4"

25°   25°

BACK   FRONT

3 1/8

2 15/16

CLOCK
BODY

SAW
CUTS

20°   1/4

BLOCK FROM WHICH CLOCK BODY IS CUT

4 7/16

3 3/4

4 5/16

BASE of CLOCK BODY

materials list
desk clock

inches

QUANTITY	DIMENSIONS T W L
1 pc.	$3^1/_8$ x $4^1/_4$ x $4^7/_{16}$

millimeters

QUANTITY	DIMENSIONS T W L
1 pc.	79 x 108 x 113

step 1 Run one edge of your wood block over your jointer so that the face in which the clock will be mounted is perpendicular to the adjacent face.

step 2 I had to be very careful about the placement of the clock on this block of wood. To the right, you'll see splits coming into the picture from the sawn end of the block. To the left you can see — very faintly — beetle tunnels in the sapwood.

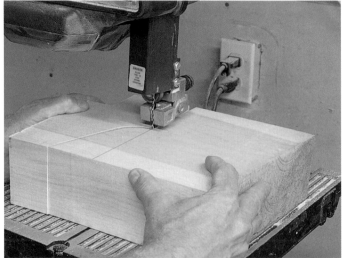

step 3 Sketch in half of the bilaterally symmetrical clock body, then cut that half on the band saw.

step 4 Use that cut half as a template for marking the other half.

step 5 Work the entire band-sawn surface of the clock body with a block plane to remove saw marks. It's much easier to do this at this stage, when the block can be easily clamped in a vise, than it is later when the sides of the clock are no longer parallel.

step 6 With the clock in position, measure the center point of the mortise in which the clock will sit.

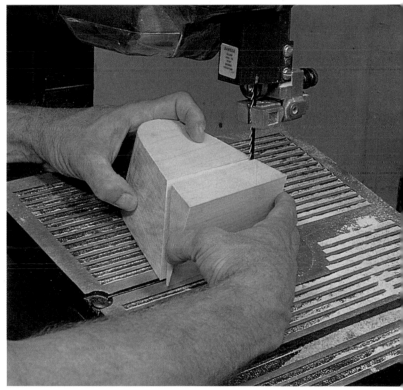

step 7 Even though I don't like spade bits, I had to use one here because I didn't have a Forstner bit of the right size, and I did pay a price for the use of that spade bit. When I was raising the bit from the hole, one of the spurs on the bottom of the bit caught on the end grain in the hole and scarred the edges. Fortunately, the clock face concealed the damage.

step 8 Set the table on your band saw at a 30° angle. Then draw a line 1¼" up from the bottom back of the clock body, and cut along that line as shown here.

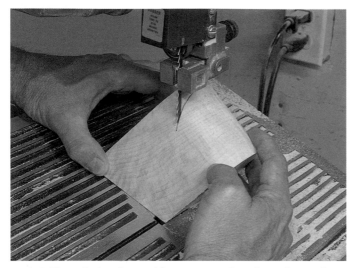

step 9 Keep the band saw table at a 30° angle and put the newly created bottom back of the clock body in place. Cut along the line as shown here.

step 10 Because it would be very difficult to draw a useful guide line on the rounded upper surface of the clock body, I followed one of the corrugations on the band-saw table as I fed the work past the blade. The band saw blade's natural angle of drift will create some error in a cut made this way, but across such a narrow width of stock the angle of drift won't create a significant problem.

step 11 This photo shows the relationship between the finished clock body and the two large pieces cut away from that body to create the finished form.

step 12 The biggest problem when you work with small, irregularly shaped stock is holding that stock securely while you work with hand tools. Here you see the clock body is suspended — not gripped — between the wooden jaws of my vise. To hold it against the action of my block plane, I've placed a small bar clamp on the outer vise jaw.

step 13 To plane the newly created back face of the clock body, hold it facedown on your bench with one jaw of a bar clamp acting as a stop. After final sanding, finish the clock body and install the clock works.

cherry shelves

My wife collects pottery, and to display her collection I've installed 24 lineal feet of cherry shelving on one

wall of our living room. The longest single section is 11'. The remainder is broken into three 4'-long

sections. The two units shown here were built to match that shelving, although on a much smaller scale.

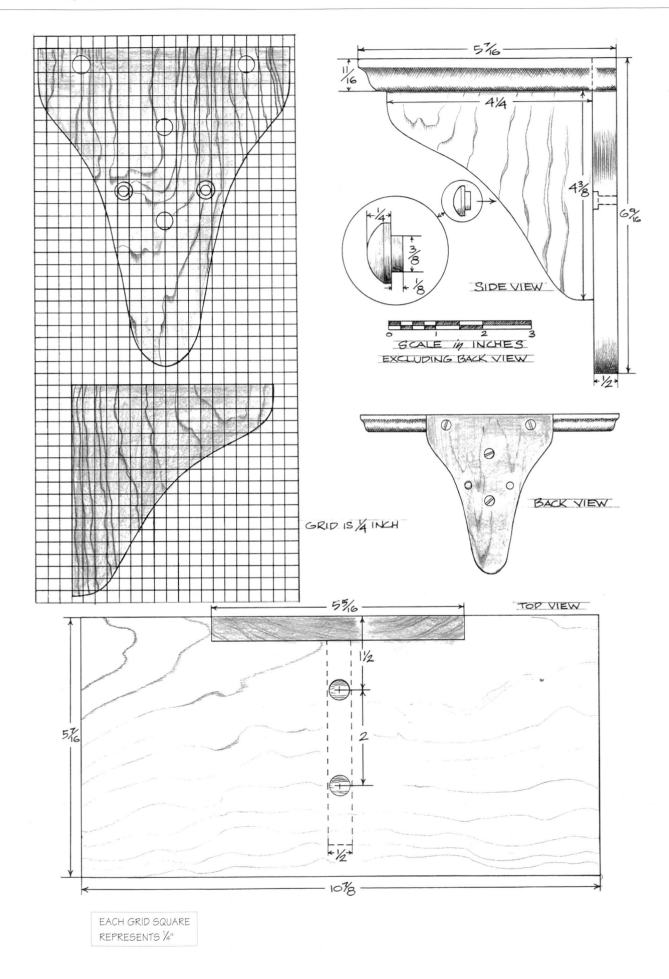

5 7/16

11/16

4 1/4

4 3/8

6 9/16

1/4

3/8

1/8

SIDE VIEW

1/2

0 1 2 3

SCALE IN INCHES
EXCLUDING BACK VIEW

BACK VIEW

GRID IS 1/4 INCH

TOP VIEW

5 5/16

1 1/2

2

1/2

5 7/16

10 7/8

EACH GRID SQUARE
REPRESENTS 1/4"

step 1 The front and back of many table saw fences, mine for example, are tightened separately. When setting the fence, measure to the blade, then measure across to the miter-gauge slot. Set this measurement at the front and back of the fence. When the front fence-to-slot measurement and the back fence-to-slot measurement agree, tighten both ends of the fence.

materials list
cherry shelves (each)

inches

ITEM	QUANTITY	DIMENSIONS T W L
Shelf	1 pc.	$^{11}/_{16}$ x $5^7/_{16}$ x $10^7/_8$
Bracket back	1 pc.	$^1/_2$ x $5^5/_{16}$ x $6^9/_{16}$
Bracket front	1 pc.	$^1/_2$ x $4^1/_4$ x $4^3/_8$
Plugs for shelf	2 pcs.	$^1/_4$ x $3^5/_8$ x $3^5/_8$
Buttons for bracket back	2 pcs.	$^3/_8$ x $^3/_8$

millimeters

ITEM	QUANTITY	DIMENSIONS T W L
Shelf	1 pc.	18 x 138 x 276
Bracket back	1 pc.	13 x 135 x 166
Bracket front	1 pc.	18 x 104 x 112
Plugs for shelf	2 pcs.	18 x 92 x 92
Buttons for bracket back	2 pcs.	10 x 10

step 2 After you've ripped and jointed the shelf material, cut it to length on your radial-arm saw. To minimize the chipping that can occur on the back side of the radial-arm saw blade, place a width of masking tape across the area to be cut.

step 3 With your block plane, dress the end-grain radial-arm saw cuts, by working from both sides toward the middle.

step 4 Install your router bit.

step 5 You'll have less trouble getting clean cuts with your router bit if you make the cuts in several passes. In this photo, the completed cut can be seen on the edge of the top shelf. The shelf below has not yet made its final pass over the router table.

step 6 A miter gauge can help you control the workpiece when you cut the end-grain edge.

step 7 To cut that end grain, place the stock so that the end to be shaped abuts the router table fence and the adjacent edge is positioned against the miter gauge (set at 0°). Push the work against the router bit at a steady and relatively brisk pace. If the work passes over the bit too slowly or if the work is stopped even for an instant while in contact with the router bit, you'll have some scorch marks to sand away from the shaped edge.

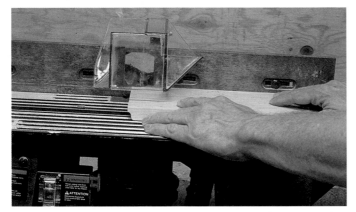

step 8 After shaping the end-grain edges, shape the long-grain edge by pushing it against the bit while pressing it back against the fence. Again, a steady and relatively brisk pace can prevent scorch marks.

step 9 The term *scrap* can be applied to material exhibiting many different kinds of defects. The 3' length of cherry shown here is larger than most scrap. It was, in fact, purchased as part of a load of material graded as *select* or better. However, this particular section of board was set aside because of a number of defects. The worst of those — a knot and a number of pitch pockets — are circled. After some judicious layout, a number of small but very usable pieces can be taken from this board and used for this project.

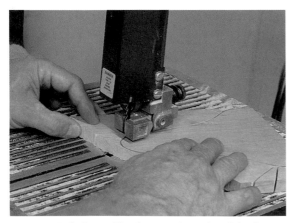

step 10 Relief cuts, like those to the right of the fingers of my right hand, make it possible to cut fairly tight radii with a ¼" blade.

step 11 I used this drill press mounted drum sander to clean up the band saw marks. The drum sander removes material much more quickly than hand sanding, but it can leave behind a hardened surface that is difficult to work with finer grits.

step 12 Mark the halfway point along the length of the shelf. Place the back of the shelf bracket back so that its center aligns with that halfway point, at the same time the back side of the bracket back aligns with the back edge of the shelf. Then, on the top of the shelf, make a line around the bracket back.

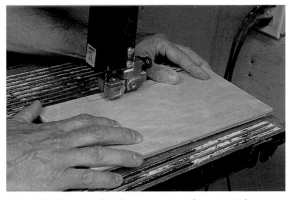

step 13 On your band saw, cut out the material you marked.

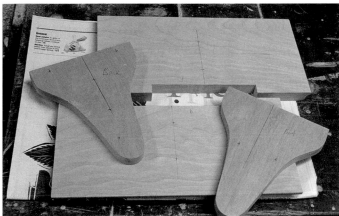

step 14 At this time, you're ready to lay out the many screw holes these shelves require. The bracket back on the left is marked to show the location of the screws that will be turned into the back of the shelf and the two screws that will be turned into the back of the bracket front. The bracket back on the right side is marked to show the location of the two screws that will be used to install the shelf onto the wall. The two shelves are marked to show the location of the screws that will fasten the shelf to the bracket front.

step 15 With a ³⁄₈" Forstner bit, drill the countersunk holes for the screw heads. These should penetrate deep enough to allow the installation of wood plugs on the top of the shelf and wood buttons on the front of the bracket back.

step 16 Then drill the through-holes with a twist bit. These holes should be large enough to permit the free passage of the screw body. I used a ³⁄₁₆" hole, just big enough for the No. 8 × 1" screws I selected.

step 17 These parts are ready for assembly.

step 18 With the shelf in your vise, place the bracket back in position and drill the holes into which the screw threads will be turned. I used a ³/₃₂" bit, which worked just fine in a relatively soft wood like cherry. You might want to select a slightly larger bit if you're building with a harder wood. After you have drilled the holes, turn in the screws that will fasten the bracket back to the shelf.

step 19 With the shelf upside down on your bench top, locate the bracket front. It should be perpendicular to both the shelf and the bracket back. I've drawn a pair of lines to help with that placement.

step 20 With your ³/₃₂" bit, drill the screw-thread holes that will fasten together the bracket front and back.

step 21 Turn the No. 8 × 1" screws into their holes.

step 22 Rotate the shelf 90° so that the back of the bracket is on your bench top. After drilling the necessary holes, turn in the wood screws to fasten the shelf to the bracket front.

step 23 Glue and tap into place the plugs that will hide the screw heads on the shelf top.

walnut box

I like making boxes. I particularly like making boxes that combine beauty and simplicity of construction. This

little box can be made in a couple of hours, and — because it's made of walnut — it will appeal to any eye.

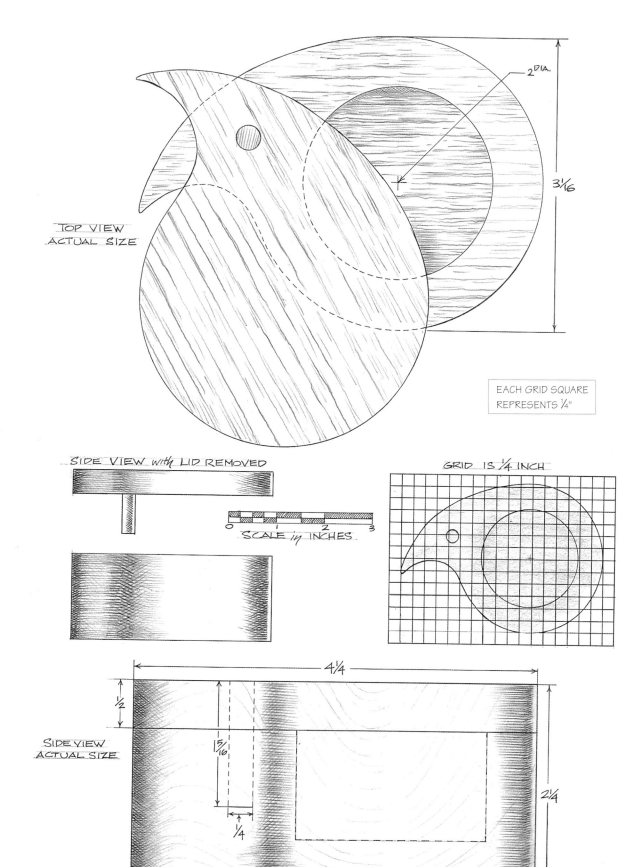

2ᴰ¹ᴬ.

3 1/16

TOP VIEW
ACTUAL SIZE

EACH GRID SQUARE
REPRESENTS 1/4"

SIDE VIEW with LID REMOVED

SCALE in INCHES

GRID IS 1/4 INCH

4 1/4

1/2

SIDE VIEW
ACTUAL SIZE

1 5/16

1/4

2 1/4

materials list
walnut box

inches

REFERENCE	QTY.	DIMENSIONS T W L
Box	1 pc.	$2^{3}/_{8}$* x $3^{1}/_{16}$ x $4^{1}/_{4}$
Dowel	1 pc.	$^{1}/_{4}$ x $1^{5}/_{16}$

*The extra thickness allows enough material for the band saw cut that separates the box and the lid.

millimeters

REFERENCE	QTY.	DIMENSIONS T W L
Box	1 pc.	61* x 77 x 108
Dowel	1 pc.	6 x 33

*The extra thickness allows enough material for the band saw cut that separates the box and the lid.

step 1 Begin by sketching the box's profile on your stock. The circle is created with a compass. The little tail is sketched in freehand.

step 2 Cut out the box on your band saw. Relief cuts around the perimeter of the box make the band-sawing process proceed smoothly.

step 3 Smooth out the band saw marks with a rasp.

step 4 Using a tri-square as a guide, mark the division between box and lid.

step 5 Separate the lid from the box on your band saw. Notice that the mark doesn't need to be drawn all the way around the box.

step 6 To plane the band-sawn bottom of the lid, create an enclosure from a bit of scrap. In this photo I've locked the lid into the enclosure with the nose of my bar clamp.

step 7 Sand the newly planed surfaces on the bottom of the lid and the top of the box by passing them over sheets of sandpaper laid flat on your bench. Keep the object you're sanding flat against the paper. If it rocks as you sand the final surface won't be flat, creating unsightly gaps between the bottom of the lid and the top of the box.

step 8 Create the body of the box with a Forstner bit. Although I would never hold in my hand a piece being drilled with a spade bit of this diameter, the Forstner bit imparts much less torque to the work. If this technique makes you uncomfortable, don't try it. I never do things in my shop that make me uncomfortable, even if I've seen other woodworkers demonstrate the techniques in their shops. A holding jig could be quickly cobbled together from a couple of clamps and some scrap lumber.

step 9 After hollowing out the box's interior, tape the box and the lid together and drill the hole for your pivot pin.

step 10 After cutting the pivot pin to length, put a bit of glue on one end and press that end up through the lid so that the pin stands about $1/32$" proud. Then sand the top of the pin flush with the top of the lid.

step 11 Sand all surfaces thoroughly.

step 12 The lid opens by rotating on the pivot pin.

figured maple box

This box was made from scrap left over after cutting out the clock shown in Project 13. At first glance the scrap didn't show much promise. The material close to the profile of the clock body was marred by a scattering of powdery post-beetle holes, and the other end of the scrap was dominated by an enormous knot. However when I cut along a line near the knot, a bit of flame figure was revealed, and this box became a setting for that figure.

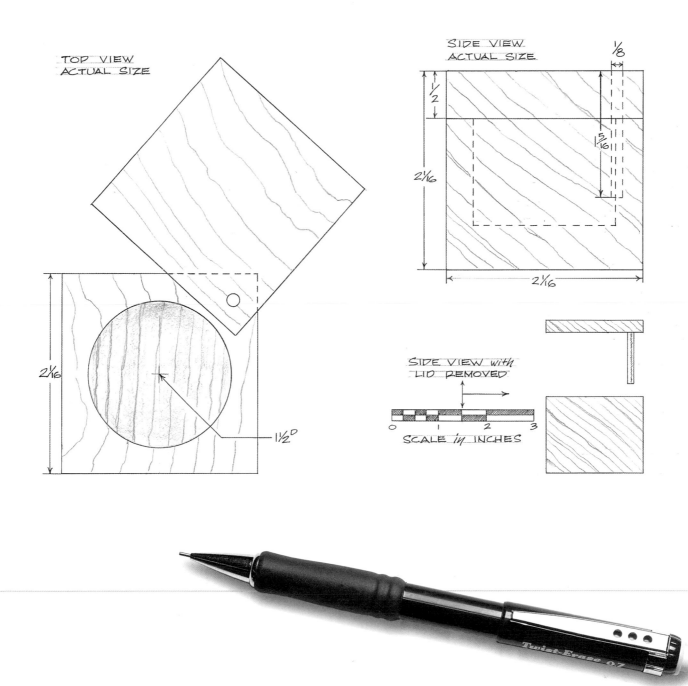

materials list
figured maple box

inches

REFERENCE	QTY.	DIMENSIONS T W L
Box	1 pc.	$2^3/_{16}$* x $2^1/_{16}$ x $2^1/_{16}$
Dowel	1 pc.	$^1/_8$ x $1^5/_{16}$

*The extra thickness allows enough material for the band saw cut that separates the box and the lid.

millimeters

REFERENCE	QTY.	DIMENSIONS T W L
Box	1 pc.	56* x 53 x 53
Dowel	1 pc.	3 x 33

*The extra thickness allows enough material for the band saw cut that separates the box and the lid.

step 1 The only way to determine the limits of a knot is to cut the material open.

step 2 I was relieved to see that the knot hadn't invaded that part of the scrap I wanted to use. I was also pleased to note the presence of a bit of flame figure on the faces of my band saw cut.

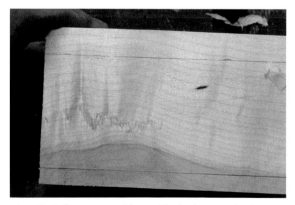

step 3 A few passes with my block plane made that flame figure more evident.

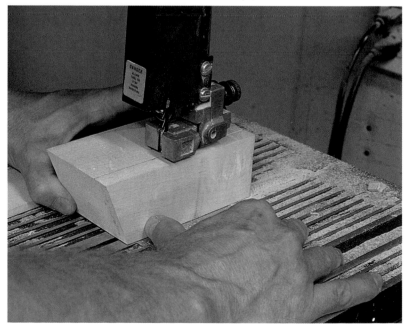

step 4 On the band saw, separate the lid material from the box material.

step 5 Lay out your box on the most attractively figured portion of your stock.

step 6 Because the box and lid are so small, it will be easier to work them with your plane if you don't first cut those parts to length.

step 7 Once the band-sawn surfaces have been planed and sanded, cut the box and lid to length.

step 8 While it is possible to plane end-grain surfaces, the tiny size of these parts would make the process very difficult. As an alternative, tape together the long-grain faces of the box and lid. Then press the end-grain surfaces against a belt sander secured to the top of your workbench.

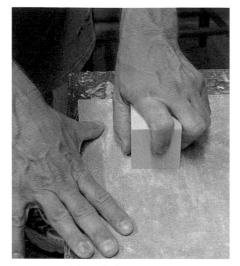

step 9 Holding the box and lid together, rub all surfaces against sandpaper laid flat on your workbench. Remember to keep the box flat against the paper as you sand, though it isn't quite as easy as it might seem.

step 10 Draw diagonals on the top of the box body to locate the center. Press the tip of your awl into this center. This awl mark will help you locate the tip of the Forstner bit.

step 11 Create the body of the box with a Forstner bit. Although I would never hold in my hand a piece being drilled with a spade bit of this diameter, the Forstner bit imparts much less torque to the work. If this technique makes you uncomfortable, don't try it. I never do things in my shop that make me uncomfortable, even if I've seen other woodworkers demonstrate the techniques in their shops. A holding jig could be quickly cobbled together from a couple of clamps and some scrap lumber.

step 12 With the box's top and bottom taped together, drill the hole into which you will fit the pivot pin.

figured maple spatula

materials list
figured maple spatula

inches

QUANTITY	DIMENSIONS T W L
1 pc.	$7/16$ x $1^{13}/16$ x $10^{11}/16$

millimeters

QUANTITY	DIMENSIONS T W L
1 pc.	11 x 46 x 272

One of the many things I like about figured maple is its ability to invigor-ate even the simplest form. Certainly no form could be simpler than that of the object shown here. Nevertheless, done in figured maple, this spatula becomes an attractive — as well as practical — kitchen implement.

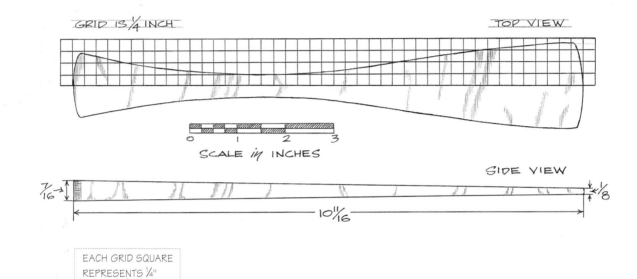

GRID IS $1/4$ INCH   TOP VIEW

SCALE *in* INCHES

SIDE VIEW

$7/16$ $1/8$

$10^{11}/16$

EACH GRID SQUARE
REPRESENTS $1/4$"

step 1 Begin by sketching the spatula's profile on the material you've selected.

step 2 Cut out that profile on your band saw.

step 3 Holding the spatula in your vise, establish a center line along the length of one edge. This is most easily done by setting your tri-square so that the blade protrudes from the head a distance that is a bit less than half the thickness of the stock. Then draw the tri-square along that stock while creating a line with a pencil point held at the end of the blade.

step 4 Mark the finish thickness of the two ends of the spatula on either side of either end of your centerline.

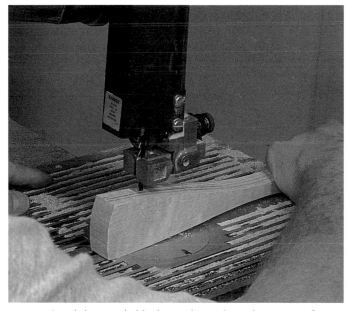

step 6 Stand the spatula blank on edge and cut the tapering faces.

step 5 Connect the marks with a straightedge flexible enough to follow the spatula's band-sawn profile. I used a ½" splint.

step 8 Use a jack plane to true the band-sawn surfaces.

step 7 In order to work the band-sawn surfaces with a plane, the stock must be fixed between stops. I found that the rips I cut off on the band saw worked very well. Those rips have been bradded to a length of scrap material.

step 9 Any tear out that escapes the jack plane can be scraped away with a butt chisel.

step 10 Refine the edges of the spatula with a rasp. Because the front and back of the spatula taper, the entire length could not be held tightly in the jaws of my vise, so I improvised: I clamped one end in my vise and rested the other end on a nail set across the jaws of the vise.

turned and band-sawn
letter opener

materials list

turned and band-sawn letter opener

This project combines two very different shaping techniques: turning and band sawing. The result is a form that couldn't be created as efficiently in any other way.

inches

QUANTITY	DIMENSIONS T W L
1 pc.	1¼ x 10½

millimeters

QUANTITY	DIMENSIONS T W L
1 pc.	32 x 267

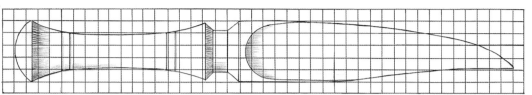

SIDE VIEW

GRIDS ARE ¼ INCH

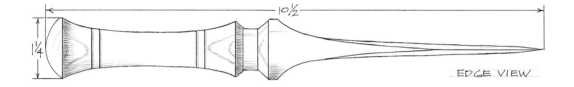

10½

1¼

EDGE VIEW

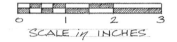

0   1   2   3

SCALE in INCHES

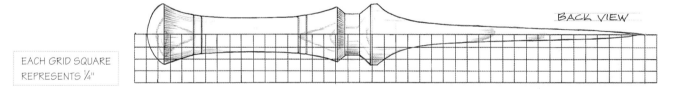

BACK VIEW

EACH GRID SQUARE REPRESENTS ¼"

step 1 Check your turning blank for defects. On this particular bit of scrap one side had a knot which I removed by ripping the stock along the pencil line.

step 2 Place one corner of your square turning stock in the notch (that runs from the front of the table to the blade) in front of your band saw blade. Hold the stock so the opposite corner of the stock aligns with the blade. Press the stock gently against the blade. Rotate the stock 90° and repeat. This identifies the centers (where the two cuts intersect) on the end grain of your stock and creates notches for the spurs on your lathe's drive center.

step 3 I built a simple jig to help me change square turning stock into octagonal stock before mounting it in the lathe. The octagonal shape approximates a turned cylinder, which makes the roughing-in of large stock a little less stressful.

step 4 With your roughing gouge, reduce the turning blank to a cylinder.

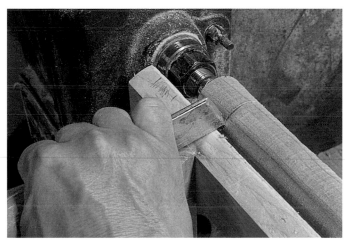

step 5 With your parting tool, mark the transition between the handle and the blade.

step 6 Mark the end of the handle with your skew. Using a parting tool, reduce the material beyond that end to approximately ⅝".

step 7 Place your skew on your tool rest with the point down and the skew resting on one corner at a 45° angle to the tool rest. Bring the skew into the work so that the point meets the work ⅛" from the end of the cut made by the parting tool. Rotate the skew into the parting-tool cut so the point peels material away and creates a radius on the end of the letter opener. Do this in several passes, each one beginning ⅛" farther back from the parting-tool cut; continue until the desired radius has been achieved.

step 8 With a fingernail gouge — ½" or ¾" — rough in the handle.

step 9 With that same fingernail gouge, rough in the shape of the blade.

step 10 Sand with a variety of grits. My sequence is 80 grit first (if necessary), 100 grit, 150 grit, then 220 grit.

step 11 Mark the locations of the decorative scorings.

step 12 Using the knife edge of your skew, create the scorings. Sand the handle once again with 220 grit.

step 13 With a straightedge flexible enough to follow the shape of the turning, establish a center line for the blade thickness. I used a length of rattan splint.

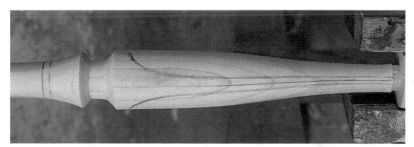

step 14 Sketch in the blade thickness.

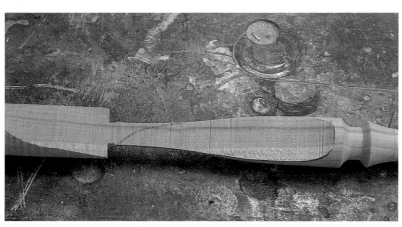

step 15 Cut the blade thickness on the band saw. I began the cut in the waste area beyond the blade tip. Notice that I stayed well outside the line in order to give myself material to rasp away later when I remove the saw marks. This operation requires a steady hand. Although the cut is made freehand, the faces of the blade must remain perpendicular to the band saw table.

step 16 Mark the tip of the blade on one of the faces created in the previous step.

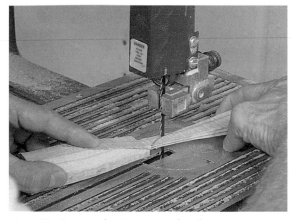

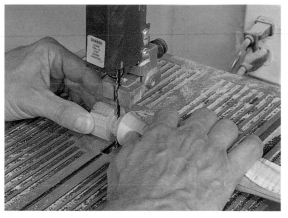

step 18 Remove the waste at the top of the handle. Finish the end with a rasp and sandpaper.

step 17 Cut out the tip on your band saw.

step 19 Clean up the band saw marks and complete the blade shaping with a rasp, followed by sandpaper.

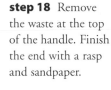

Mark's working environment features a custom-built lathe table which includes foot rests and knee pads placed to suit Mark's legs.

Mark Burhans
a master of miniature

When we think about professional woodworkers, we often imagine men and women who take truckloads of lumber and transform them into chairs, beds, tables and cabinets. However, in the woodworking world a surprising number of men and women make a living by taking little bits and pieces many would view as scrap and transforming those bits and pieces into goods that can command significant prices. In the following profile, which originally ran in *Woodwork* magazine, I look at the life of one such woodworker: Mark Burhans of Athens, Ohio.

Mark Burhans is perched in his custom-made cockpit, body bent over the lathe, hands making subtle and precise adjustments. A sudden stream of chips arcs neatly to the floor. His shoulders shift as his hands take a new position, and another stream of chips leaps from the skew. Shoulders swaying rhythmically, he leans toward the lathe, wrists rotating gently, body twisting slightly at the waist. A single shaving, 6" long, sprays from the work, briefly taking flight, then coming to rest on his leg.

Captured in the enormous bulk of his lathe, the subject of his efforts is a mere scrap of wood, seemingly too small to be the focus of such intense concentration, too tiny and insubstantial. This is, in fact, a description that can be applied to nearly all the work that emerges from Mark's basement shop, to all the bud vases, pins and chess pieces. It is all built to a diminutive scale.

Why not full-size woodwork? Why not highboys or beds or tables and chairs?

There are many reasons. First, Mark has labored for years to create a product that is recognizably his own, to create an identifiable Mark Burhans market niche. Since he started small, he has felt a need to remain small. There is also the matter of personal taste. Although he has made full-size work he takes more pleasure in the production of intimate, miniature work. Then there is material. Since he's chosen to work primarily in spalted maple, the output of his shop is limited by the size of available spalted wood. Mark explains it this way: "I make some larger pieces, but it's really hard to find big spalted stock with good figure, because spalted wood is in the process of deterioration and quite often where you have good spalting, right next to that you've got rotted wood." Finally, perhaps most important, there is the matter of shop size. By almost any standards, Mark's shop is tiny, and in Mark's words, "There's a kind of symbiotic relationship between the size of my shop and the size of the work I do. There just isn't room to do big stuff."

Although we arrive early in the day, the air is thick with incipient August heat. My T-shirt clings to my back and shoulders. I feel sweat beading my forehead.

Mark Burhan's 1920s-era home stands on a quiet, tree-lined street in Athens, Ohio, not far from the campus of Ohio University. As I mount the steps to Mark's front porch, I hear the shrill voices of children somewhere in the neighborhood.

I lower my armload of photo gear to the porch floor and knock on the front door. It opens quickly and Mark steps outside. We shake hands as I introduce myself and my photographer, Garry Frazier.

Mark is in his early forties with a full beard and casually arranged hair into which a little gray has begun to creep. He's wearing a T-shirt and jeans, which is something of a uniform for woodworkers in Ohio. We talk briefly about the weather. I then notice a cardboard carton of fist-size wood blocks on the porch. Each block is marked with hard-edged gray lines against a cream-colored background,

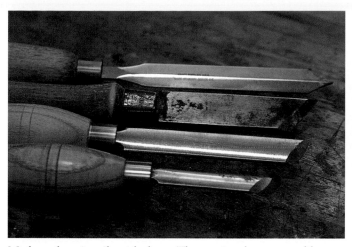

Mark works primarily with skews. The turning demonstrated here required only a parting tool and these three skews.

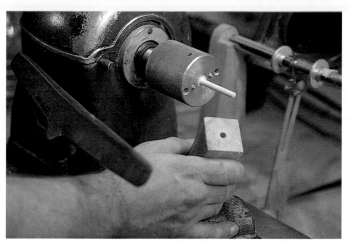

His turning stock is placed on a thin wood spigot.

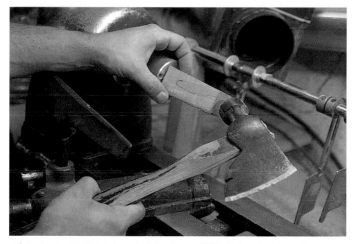

After the mortise in the stock is slid over the spigot, the stock is tapped into place on the drive center's spurs.

Diameters at either end of the turning are set with a parting tool.

the distinctive appearance of spalted maple. I point to the box. "Where do you get your spalted stuff?"

Mark laughs. "Anywhere. People know I use it, so they just drop it off."

I reach into the box and pull out a couple of blocks. For a few minutes, we talk about spalting and about the availability of figured wood. Then I ask to see his shop.

"Let's go around to the side door," Mark suggests. "It'll be easier to get your stuff in."

We pick up the photo gear, leave the porch, and enter the side yard of Mark's house through a gate in a 6'-high wood fence.

"When we bought the house, I realized that if I had a shop in the house itself, I wouldn't be paying rent. Plus it

would be a short drive to work," Mark says.

The side door of the house opens onto a narrow flight of steps leading down to Mark's basement workshop. The corners and clearances near the door are tight, particularly when your arms are full of camera gear. Maneuvering carefully, we make our way down the stairs into the basement.

The first room is long and narrow, maybe 8' in width. A 1950s Atlas lathe occupies one wall. A Jet band saw stands near the base of the stairs. More space is consumed by a couple of storage cabinets. With the addition of three men, the room becomes quite crowded. I edge to one side as Mark sidles past me.

"Just put your stuff anywhere." Mark gestures at the tiny room.

I lower the photo gear to the floor. Stepping over it, I follow Mark as he moves into the next room, which is even smaller. Here, much of the space is taken up by a large, heavily made workbench and some attached storage shelves. Mark points to a doorway on my right. "There's a table saw in there."

I stick my head through the door. Yes, there is a table saw, and no space for anything else. I can't imagine cutting sheet goods on that saw in the tiny room.

Woodworkers are made, not born. Although some men and women have more manual and aesthetic potential than others, there are no prodigies. Excellence in the shop requires years of study, discipline and practice. Mark is no exception.

His journey began at Antioch College in Yellow Springs, Ohio, where he decided to study architecture. Unfortunately, there was no architecture program at Antioch. He decided, then, to leave Yellow Springs and begin his education by starting with what he saw as an architectural basic: home construction. "I wanted to see how houses were built from the ground up," he explains. "I thought that would make me a better architect."

In 1976, he left Antioch and headed for Washington, DC, which was then experiencing a building boom. There he took a job as a carpenter's helper. He quickly moved up the woodworking ladder, finding a job in a cabinet shop near Capitol Hill, where he had the opportunity to work with some highly skilled cabinetmakers. He discovered he liked working in the shop, even though that particular shop focused on architectural woodwork — staircases, plywood shells, cornice work — as opposed to the smaller, more intimate woodworking that would eventually become his trademark. As he worked in this Washington, DC, cabinet shop, he realized there was an artistic side to his nature, and he began to think about going back to school to develop this potential, this time with the intention of studying woodwork.

At that same time, the field of American woodworking was taking off. *Fine Woodworking* magazine was in the process of becoming a national institution. Weekend workshops and college-level woodworking programs were proliferating like weeds. In 1979, shortly after marrying his longtime fiancée Hilarie, Mark began to look for a school that would allow him to develop his interest in woodworking.

"I quit my job and went on this road trip to search for a woodworking school, and the first place I went I ended up going: Indiana University of Pennsylvania in Indiana, Pennsylvania." The university had just hired a Rochester Institute of Technology graduate, Chris Weiland, to put together a woodworking program. Mark explains, "Chris was then, and still is, a very enthusiastic teacher. He brought in people like Stephen Hogbin; Robert Meadows, a lute maker from New York and Robert Strini, a wood sculptor who does free-form laminated wood structures.

"It was a really good program that gave us a firm foundation in tool techniques. It also included a very rigorous grounding in aesthetics. 'Why do you want it to look like this?' that kind of thing. In an art school (like Indiana University of Pennsylvania), you bring an idea to a professor and he shoots it down. It can be very frustrating. But it does teach you how to see."

In 1983, after three years in the program, Mark graduated and began to search for a way to make a name for himself in the woodworking field, looking early on at woodturning. "I was impressed by the fact that a turner could take a raw hunk of wood and use a single tool through the entire process, whereas with other forms of woodworking, you have to go from tool to tool to tool."

He encountered the work of Stephen Hogbin who was then doing split-turnings (turnings that are sawn lengthwise after being removed from the lathe), and inspired by this work, Mark began to experiment with the notion of cutting into the turned form, an experimentation that eventually led to the work he is doing today. "The thing about turning is that it's so symmetrical, so round. Ever since I saw Stephen Hogbin's work, I've kind of kept that in my mind: What can I do to interrupt that roundness, to change it a little, to make it a little bit different?"

It's tough to make a living as a woodworker, particularly when the focus of your business isn't custom work but is, instead, a line of original designs. This difficulty can be addressed in many ways, one of which is controlling expenses during the inevitable early years of struggle.

In this connection, Mark and his wife got a break almost immediately. Just as he graduated from college, his mother- and father-in-law, both professors at Ohio University, decided to move to Malaysia to teach there, and they offered their home to Hilarie and Mark to use free, with utilities paid. Since both Mark and his wife had grown up in Athens, they were pleased to use that city as a home base for Mark's career. With some money Mark borrowed from his parents he purchased equipment and materials and started playing around with ideas.

Another component in the financial mix is a spouse who is willing to work.

Creating a Chess Set

Every turner has a chess-set story. For some, the story describes the creation of a chess set that the turner has actually made. For others, the story describes a chess set that the turner may someday make; if there's time, if there's a buyer, if the right material becomes available. Mark's chess set, done in walnut and maple, was created so that his chess-set story would describe something he had actually made.

He began by solving the problem of the knight. Every other piece in a turner's chess set can be created entirely on the lathe, but the knight, the only piece that must be asymmetrical because of its need to represent a horse, poses special problems for the turner. Mark, therefore, began the design process with this piece, incorporating sawn turnings that were already a prominent feature of his work.

He then began to lay out the other pieces, designing them around four principles: First, to achieve the necessary contrast, he built the dark pieces primarily of walnut and the light pieces primarily of maple. Second, he decided to assemble the pieces from a series of small turned disks and cylinders arranged on a central spigot. Third, each piece was assembled of parts made of components that, for each piece, alternated between walnut and maple. And perhaps most important, because he saw chess as a game in which war and fantasy were central elements, he created a design that "captured its military origins and its Wizard of Oz feel."

Although the work was spread out over a year, Mark estimates he had only four weeks of actual shop time: one week to create the prototypes and two weeks to make the actual turnings.

With a smaller skew, he turns the vases.

Then with a wide skew, the blank is rough-turned to a cylinder.

When the turning is complete, it's cut from the spigot with the skew's knife edge.

The completed turning is then slid from the spigot.

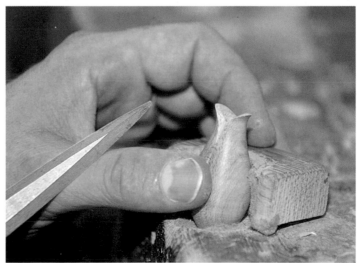

The two lips are roughed in on a sanding belt.

The lips are finished using a file.

Mark's wife quickly found a job in Athens running a home day care. "That's been true all along," Mark explains. "In order to survive, we've both had to work." In addition, Mark and his wife have both played in a bluegrass band for many years and at one time ran a catering business.

Eventually, like almost everyone in the craft business, Mark tried retail shows, and like almost everyone who tries them he experienced little real success. "I found out pretty early on that retail shows were tough. My neighbors always seemed to be doing a little better than me, or they would say: 'You should have been here last year. I don't know what it is about this year, but last year was great.' Eventually I got into the first Rosen Show (a wholesale show formally known as the Buyers Market of American Craft) at Valley Forge in 1983, and I've been doing the Rosen Shows ever since. Those shows, as well as trying to keep my lifestyle simple, have made it work for me."

Like so many other craftsmen, Mark discovered that the show circuit, whether retail or wholesale, is a tough way to generate real income, and he has now reached a point in his career at which he tries to do the fewest-possible number of shows. "While they can increase your revenue," he explains, "your profit goes down. There's booth fees, downtime to do the show, travel expenses. For instance, when I do the Philadelphia show I lose a whole week, more than that if I figure the time to prep for the show."

Mark has also explored other outlets for his work. One of those is a shop in Athens called the Court Street Collection, at which his work has sold well. In addition, he now sells through a wholesale Internet company. Plus, he does a fair amount of commissioned work. For example, he recently made a number of gavels to be given as gifts by the economics department at Ohio University. And, as one of the few professional turners in his area, he is often asked to do restoration turnings.

After a resurrection that lasted throughout the 1970s and the 1980s, the American craft movement has begun to show signs of decay. Although there are now more retail and wholesale shows than at any time in the past, exhibitors often find themselves with less money in their pockets at the close of these shows, the same shows that, for many in the craft field, had previously been the foundations of their yearly incomes. As a result, some very highly skilled designer/craftsmen are looking longingly at more conventional jobs that offer insurance and retirement benefits, better wages, fewer hours, more security.

This drop-off in show income may reflect a change in the public's taste. In the information age, the handcrafted artifact may have lost some of its appeal. This is a perceptual shift that Mark finds very troubling. "You see stuff that's not well designed and not well made. Or it's designed in such a way that minimum-wage people can be hired to put it together. It's devoid of all artistic content, of a heart. And this stuff is selling like crazy."

In part, Mark blames designer/craftsmen themselves for this situation. "We have a responsibility to educate people so they can see why this [handcrafted work] is special, why you should buy it."

But in spite of such frustrations, Mark remains positive about his work. "On a day-to-day level I'm not discouraged at all. I'm still having fun. I love going out in my shop every day. It's a great life."

It is also a life he finds artistically challenging. "What I'm doing every day is looking at that line, looking at that silhouette. I'm trying to create this beautiful curve. There's something fulfilling about that process, something Zen-like. Sometimes I think about what I'm doing and I think, 'Man. What a life.' I would never want to give it up entirely, but it's a tough way to make a living."

Selling Craftwork on Television

We don't think of television as a marketing tool for individual designer/craftsmen, but QVC, a shopping channel, has developed a program that makes that a possibility, and in 1997, they offered the services of that program to 50 artisans from the state of Ohio. Potential participants were chosen from a larger number who exhibited their work at a one-day craft show held at the Ohio State Fairgrounds in Columbus, Ohio. For a modest $25 booth fee these designer/craftsmen earned the opportunity to show their work to QVC representatives.

It was, Mark explains, a very unusual show. "I set up a booth and showed my work, but there were only three customers — all from QVC. They walked around and looked at everybody's stuff. Then we took our booths down and went home."

Once he had been selected, Mark began his preparations. In order to qualify, he had to have $10,000 worth of merchandise, an enormous amount for someone accustomed to working primarily alone in very limited production runs. "At that time, I had an assistant working with me, a friend of mine — Jeff Graham — who came in one day a week or so. He did a lot of the detail work, the hand-filing for example — so well that I couldn't tell whether an individual piece had been done by him or by me.

"And my daughter did all the administrative work. All the pins had to go on cards. You've got to put the pin-back in. You've got put the little glass tube in, and the suction cup. And they go in the box. You've got to put the tape on, the label. She did all that stuff."

Once the work was ready, another problem surfaced. On the same day Mark was scheduled to appear on the show, he had a booking for his bluegrass band, a booking he had accepted some months earlier. "So I hired my sister-in-law, who's really good at marketing, and we presented her as part of the company. She was my agent in that particular instance."

Although he didn't sell out, his QVC experience was successful, and Mark was impressed with the treatment he and his work received from the television network. "The QVC people were wonderful folks," he explains, "very professional, very considerate."

Working with Spalted Wood

Mark's approach to the turning process is impacted by the fact that he works with spalted wood. "It's become a market niche for me, but it can be difficult to work with because the figure isn't always where you want it. A lot of times you'll look at a rough piece and see the figure on the surface and you'll say, 'Wow. That's going to be great.' But then you'll turn all the figure away getting down to your shape.

"It's like cutting a gemstone, because you want to get the figure right, centered in the piece. Sometimes, when you're working with a larger piece, you may not know about the good figure in the center and you have to keep working to get that figure to show.

"It often happens — amazingly enough — that a piece doesn't look like much at first, but after you've turned it and you've stopped the lathe, you'll discover this great figure. It's one of the wonderful things about spalted wood."

Although he delights in the figure spalted wood presents, Mark's focus is on form, and he won't modify shape in order to take advantage of figure, at least not on a conscious level.

The spalted maple vases are placed on pegs before finishing.

This is a finished pin, complete with flower.

These tiny objects are typical of Mark's production.

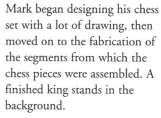

Mark began designing his chess set with a lot of drawing, then moved on to the fabrication of the segments from which the chess pieces were assembled. A finished king stands in the background.

INDEX